Salt, Light and Cities on Hills

Evangelism, Social Action
and the Church

How do they relate
to each other?

MELVIN TINKER

EP BOOKS
Faverdale North
Darlington
DL3 0PH, England

web: http://www.epbooks.org

e-mail: sales@epbooks.org

EP Books are distributed in the USA by:
JPL Distribution
3741 Linden Avenue Southeast
Grand Rapids, MI 49548
E-mail: orders@jpldistribution.com
Tel: 877.683.6935

British Library Cataloguing in Publication Data available

ISBN 978-1-78397-043-8

For Lee and Scott
Valued Friends and Gospel Partners

CONTENTS

Foreword

About ten years ago, I received a phone call from the then Principal of Oak Hill College, Professor David Peterson, asking whether I would be interested in applying for a lectureship in 'Evangelical Public Theology.' Looking back, I'm not entirely convinced David was sure what 'public theology' entailed (and at that time I certainly didn't!), but he was a visionary leader who recognised that a British theological college training men and women for pastoral ministry, needed a teaching post which addressed 'public theology' issues. What David and I did grasp even then, was that one of the fundamental areas that Evangelical public theology would have to concern itself with, was the vexed question of the relationship between evangelism and social action. It had been a constant source of discussion and sometimes heated debate with theological students and staff during my time at *UCCF: The CU Movement*, and I knew its 'hot potato' status.

Now, with ten years of having taught a final year undergraduate course at Oak Hill College called Evangelical Public Theology, I have much better grasp of what the subject is, the literature available on it, and the differing 'models' available to evangelical Christians: models determined by subtly different exegeses, biblical and systematic theologies. Moreover, I am more convinced than ever of the importance and applicability of Evangelical Public theology for those entering gospel ministry. One of the main reasons for this conviction is a recognition that those in pastoral ministry need to grapple with this fundamental relationship between evangelism and social action. How one perceives the relationship will play a determining role not only in the shape of one's ministry, but the people who are being ministered to.

During my early days of teaching, I often struggled to articulate to people what Evangelical Public theology was. However, two questions that Melvin Tinker had asked (now contained in one of the chapters of this book) were really helpful in my communication as to what it was all about, "What do the people of God owe to the ungodly? How are Christians to live out the present in light of the future?" I had come across Melvin's work previously while I had been the managing editor of the theological journal *Themelios*. I also knew that he has been Vicar of St John's Newland for some time and I had personally benefitted from his sermons available on the web, some of which had been written up as short books. Whether it was his journal articles or sermons, I always found his articles to be thoughtful and challenging, and displaying an independency of thought based on where he thought biblical exegesis was taking him.

And so to this present volume. Much of this material has been available in one form or another over the last decade and now helpfully joined together into a more structured form. What you have here is Melvin's own statement on the evangelism/social action question. What is to be appreciated is that Melvin, like all good theologians, realises the need to bring to bear a number of disciplines in coming to answers on some of his questions. So we are given the historical context of where we have come from, the theological questions that need to be addressed, and the way that the Bible construes the relationship between evangelism and social action. As is typical with Melvin's writing, and because the Bible is his ultimate authority, he is not afraid to criticise the 'great and good' of the evangelical world (wherever they are coming from on the spectrum) if he thinks exegesis has gone awry. He is also bold enough (and creative enough) to take some much-discussed passages (like the good Samaritan, and the Sermon on the Mount), and give us his own exegesis and interpretation of them. While one may not agree with every decision he makes, one definite characteristic of his understanding of these texts is how the Old Testament background is seminal in understanding these

New Testament passages. After reading this book, many I know will see these New Testament passages from a fresh perspective and will, I hope, be persuaded of Melvin's overall thesis.

Above all, what has struck me most in reading this book is that Melvin really is a true scholar-pastor. One of the constant problems I have had in teaching Evangelical Public theology is pointing my students to good examples of conservative evangelical churches *in the UK* who are 'practicing what they are preaching' when it comes to the proper biblical relationship between evangelism, social action and the church. Too often we have to look across the Atlantic (and beyond) for examples, and in lots of ways the cultural difference between the States (or Australia) and the UK means that these examples can be lost in translation. Therefore I was especially encouraged by Melvin's final chapter, and the one I had not seen before, which not only was personal and heartfelt, but showed how under Melvin's leadership, St John's has attempted to 'model the model' of evangelism and social action that Melvin has discerned from Scripture.

Of course, there are lots of detailed questions that are thrown up both in this final chapter and in the earlier ones (one for me at least is how Melvin's 'Anglicanism' informs his thinking on all these issues). I hope though that the reader can see the vision that Melvin has presented here, a vision rooted in Scripture and grounded in the lived reality of church life. I hope that people will read this book, be challenged and provoked by it, and be encouraged that there are British churches that are acting as salt, light, and cities on hills.

Dr Daniel Strange
Academic Vice Principal,
Tutor in Culture, Religion and Public Theology
Oak Hill College, London

Introduction

Present Concerns

Augustine prefaces his magnum opus, *The City of God*, with an explanation of its purpose, namely, 'The task of defending the glorious City of God against those who prefer their own gods to the Founder of that City'. Augustine presents the City of God 'both as it exists in this world of time, a stranger among the ungodly, living by faith, and as it stands in the security of its everlasting seat.'

Here is the tension between the City of God and its present opponents on the one hand, contrasted with its glorious future on the other. It is this tension of living between the 'now and the not yet' which creates the problem of how Christians are to relate to society. What do the people of God owe to 'the ungodly'? How are Christians to live in the present in the light of the future? These questions especially become acute when we come to the matter of the relationship between evangelism and social involvement.

In his *Issues Facing Christians Today*, Dr John Stott writes: 'It is exceedingly strange that any followers of Jesus Christ should ever need to ask whether social involvement was their concern, and that controversy should have blown up over the relationship between evangelism and social responsibility. For it is evident that in his public ministry Jesus both "went about ... teaching ... and preaching" (Matt 4:2; 9:35) and "went about doing good and healing" (Acts 10:38). In consequence Evangelism and social concern have been intimately related to one another throughout the history of the church ... Christian people have often engaged

in both activities quite unselfconsciously, without feeling the need
to define what they were doing or why.'[1]

More recently, Dr Jonathan Chaplin, the Director of The Kirby
Laing Institute for Christian Ethics (KLICE) has gone so far as
to say that regarding the relationship between evangelism, social
action and the Gospel there really is nothing more to discuss; such
'either/or' dichotomies are now passé: 'I won't attempt to restate
the case that has been compellingly made over many decades by
a succession of distinguished evangelical theologians, that a truly
biblical faith calls the church to be fully engaged in all aspects of
cultural, social and political life—that the 'Gospel' actually found
on Jesus' lips (see Luke 4:18–19), unlike the one still too often
found on ours, thrusts us out into the world to be servants of
healing, justice and peace. Nor am I going to rehearse the tired
old debate over the relative priorities of "evangelism" and "social
action", the very framing of which obscures the fundamental point
that "proclaiming the Gospel of the Kingdom"—the only kind
of evangelism Jesus engaged in—inescapably includes what we
today call "social action" as a constitutive element and not just a
"consequence" (still less an optional extra).'[2]

Dr Chaplin may be rather premature in his pronouncements
and certainly his comments have been met with a sharp and robust
response from Professor Paul Helm, 'This looks remarkably like
a call for the church unitedly to participate, as a fundamental
matter of the gospel of Christ, in agreed programmes of social
action. Its reference to the "compelling" work by "distinguished
evangelical theologians" could be understood as an attempt to pre-
empt debate. How crass to go against such a powerful trend! How
could this trend possibly be gainsaid? He claims that there is no
alternative, and that any discussion is nothing but words. But of
course there is plenty to be discussed.'[3]

Helm is quite correct, there is plenty to discuss as well as there
being plenty which is controversial. The controversy does not centre
on *whether* Christians should engage in social action which can
be understood as, 'acts to improve the physical, psychological and
social welfare of people'[4] but *how* that involvement should express
itself and upon what theological basis it ought to proceed. Robert

K. Johnstone observes: 'That evangelicals should be involved socially has become a foregone conclusion ... but how and why evangelicals are to involve themselves in society have proven to be more vexing questions. That they are to be involved brings near unanimity; how that involvement takes shape and what is its Christian motivation bring only debate.'[5]

On one side of the debate may be placed Dr Timothy Keller; 'The ministry of mercy is not just a means to the end of evangelism. Word and deed are equally necessary, mutually interdependent and inseparable ministries, each carried out with the single purpose of the spread of the kingdom of God.'[6] On the other side is Gary Meadors who argues, 'Jesus did not call Paul or present day Christians to a primary task of changing the world-system, but to evangelise individuals, to teach them all things he commanded, and to recognise that Satan is the "god of this world" and that our only hope for ultimate political correction is Jesus' second advent.'[7] But he is equally insistent that: 'We do not disagree that we should have compassion for starving people and for those who suffer from political injustice.'

Answers to questions of priority and motivation in evangelism and social action are inevitably shaped by the theological framework in which they are viewed. It is understandable that some evangelicals have strongly reacted against theological models which, in their eyes, are remarkably reminiscent of the 'social gospel' which wreaked havoc in many Western churches from the late 19th century throughout the 1930s and well into the 1960s, not least when definitions of what constitutes the 'Kingdom of God' seemed far removed from the way the New Testament writers use the term. Such a warning was issued by the late Sir Norman Anderson at the 1967 National Anglican Evangelical Conference (NEAC) at Keele University: 'There is a sense in which that Kingdom is already a present reality, for the King is already on his throne, waiting till all things are put under his feet ... But is there a wider sense in which one can think of the Kingdom as advanced wherever the will of the King is done, even by those who do not give Him personal allegiance? This, it seems to me, is dangerous ground, for we cannot regard the Kingdom of God as having materialised in a factory for example, merely because social justice and harmony reign therein ... The Evangelical holds no brief for the so called "social gospel", for society, as such, cannot be "redeemed" or "baptised into Christ"... But it can be reformed.'[8]

How, then, are evangelicals to react when they read such a statement as this: 'All the earth is the Lord's and so we trace the Spirit at work *beyond* the Church, especially in movements that make for human dignity and liberation.'[9]? Anxiety and caution will be expressed by some and disdain and outright opposition by others. The danger, however, for the more conservative evangelical is *over*-reaction, a concern raised by Ranald Macaulay when he writes of the move in some quarters to 'place exclusive emphasis on evangelism.'[10]

Is it possible to co-ordinate evangelism and social action in such a way that it reflects faithfully the pattern of the New Testament, enabling each to reinforce the other while avoiding the extremes of exclusive gospel proclamation on the one hand and collapsing evangelism into social action on the other? How has the present situation of tension and controversy amongst evangelicals on this issue come about? Are there lessons which we can learn from our evangelical forebears? How does what they believed and acted contrast with their 21st century theological offspring? What might a biblically shaped and theologically informed co-ordination between evangelistic activity and social action look like on the ground in 21st century Britain? These are some of the questions we shall be exploring in this book in the hope of moving beyond caricatured, entrenched positions to a better rounded and clearly recognisable evangelical appreciation.[11]

Accordingly, the book is divided into three related sections. The first part surveys the different stances taken by evangelicals towards the relation between evangelism and social involvement—both past and present and offering some critical reflections. The middle section involves providing some exegetical groundwork for what is hoped is a well rounded understanding of this relationship which is faithful to the teaching of Jesus in particular. This will also involve a testing of the proposed model by looking at the life of the early church in the book of Acts. The final chapter is more personal; indicating what applying these principles might look like on the ground in my own ministerial context in trying to 'reach the unreached'.

ENDNOTES

1. John R. W. Stott, *Issues Facing Christians Today* (Basingstoke: Marshall Pickering, 1984) p. 3

2. Jonathan Chaplin, KLICE comment: http://tyndalehouse

3. Professor Paul Helm, http://paulhelmsdeep.blogspot.co.uk/

4. This definition is put forward by John Woodhouse, 'Evangelism and Social responsibility' in B. G. Webb (Ed), *Christians in Society,* (Explorations 3, Lancer, 1988), p. 5.

5. Robert K. Johnstone, *Evangelicals at an Impasse: Biblical Authority in Practice* (Atlanta: John Knox, 1979) p. 79

6. Tim Keller, *Ministries of Mercy, The Call of the Jericho Road* (Phillipsburg, NJ: P&R, 1997), p. 106

7. Gary T. Meadors, 'John R. W. Stott on Social Action', *Grace Theological Journal* 1/2 (1980), p. 146

8. J. N. D. Anderson, 'Christian Worldliness—the need and limits of Christian Involvement', *Guidelines,* J. I. Packer (Ed), (CPAS 1967), p. 231.

9. Nigel Wright, *The Radical Evangelical* (SPCK 1996), p. 112.

10. Ranald Macaulay, 'The Great Commissions', *Cambridge Papers* 2/7 (1998)

11. Some of the material included in this book is a development of two major public lectures: The 1999 London Evangelical Library Lecture, 'Reversal or Betrayal? Evangelicals and Socio-Political Involvement in the 20th Century', in *Evangelical Concerns*, Melvin Tinker, (Fearn, Ross-shire: Christian Focus, 2001) and the 2006 John Wenham Lecture for the Tyndale Fellowship, 'The Servant Solution—The Co-ordination of Evangelism and Social Action' in *Transforming the World?*, Ed. Jamie Grant and Dewi Hughes (Nottingham: Apollos, 2009).

1

All our Yesterdays

A brief history of Evangelicals, Evangelism and Social Action

Kathleen Heasman documents how Evangelicals in the 19th century and the earlier part of the 20th century were significantly involved in social action and comments that they 'were all agreed upon salvation by faith and the infallibility and overriding importance of the Scriptures'[1] William Wilberforce, Elizabeth Fry, George Müller, Henry Venn and Anthony Ashley-Cooper are just some of the more notable names which read like a veritable 'Who's Who' of evangelical social activists who played an unquestioned part in securing anti-slavery legislation, penal reform, improving factory working conditions and the care of needy orphans in a society desperately requiring change.

In the United States Charles Finney was not only vigorous in promoting his own brand of revivalism, but reforming work as well, so that in his twenty-third lecture on Revival he could write: 'The great business of the church is to reform the world. The Church of Christ was originally organised to be a body of reformers. The very profession of Christianity implies the profession and virtually an oath to do all that can be done for the universal reformation of the world.' One of the followers of Finney who took this call to heart was Theodore Weld, who subsequently devoted his life to the struggle against slavery.

15

The shift

There then appeared to be two major shifts which took place in the first two decades of the 20th century which marked a significant departure from the stance of earlier evangelicals towards evangelism and social involvement.

According to Arthur Johnston [2] the first critical change took place between 1900 and 1910 when there was a significant change in emphasis from evangelism to social action. Under the influence of theological liberalism, the leadership of the youth missionary movements had broken away from the evangelicalism of the 19th century. Here the 'social gospel' began to blossom into full flower with the responsibility of the Christian being seen as primarily working with God to bring about his kingdom on earth in the present social order. Johnston notes how in 1909 J. H. Oldham called on what was to become the Student Christian Movement (SCM) to consider the social conditions which deny 'to our fellow men ... their share in the Fatherhood of God'. [3]

This change, according to Johnston, involved far more than incorporating a new element into missions, namely, that of social action, for 'Evangelical missions have always been "holistic" in the biblical sense and they have always sought the welfare of "the whole man" not just his soul.' [4] In other words, previously evangelism had inspired and entailed social action and reforms, but now there had been a major theological shift so that social action began to *replace* the position previously occupied by evangelism itself.

However, between about 1910 and the late 1930s, the second major shift occurred as Evangelicals seemed to be less concerned with social issues in marked contrast to their evangelical forebears of the 19th century. At least in part this could be seen as a reaction (some would say over-reaction), to the liberal theological developments which were taking place at the time in the form of the so-called 'Social Gospel' espoused by Walter Rauschenbusch, a Baptist minister and Professor of Church History at Rochester Seminary. In *Christianity and the Social Crisis*, published in 1907, he defined the Kingdom of God as 'a reconstruction of society on a Christian basis', contrasting the 'old evangel of the saved soul' with the 'new evangel of the Kingdom of God' which was primarily a matter not of getting souls into heaven, but 'transforming life on earth into the harmony of heaven'.[5] For Rauschenbusch the 'essential purpose of Christianity' was to 'transform human society into the Kingdom of God by regenerating all human relationships.'[6] It was the reaction against this kind of teaching that led many Evangelicals to distance themselves from anything which looked remotely like it. Such considerations, when combined with a growing pessimism about the ability of society to make moral progress (a pessimism exacerbated both by the experience of the First World War and premillennialist teaching), make the disengagement by many Evangelicals from social involvement, while being regrettable, nonetheless understandable.

On the wider ecclesiastical scene the social gospel movement became firmly entrenched in the ecumenical movement as embodied in the World Council of Churches from which Evangelicals were becoming further and further removed.

The 1960s saw new developments amongst Evangelicals which led to modifications in their views of mission, evangelism and social action, which some have argued now run parallel to those of the ecumenical movement itself.[7]

The congress on the Church's Worldwide Mission at Wheaton, Illinois in 1966 was called in a conscious reaction against the direction in which the WCC was moving. The paper on social responsibility entitled, 'Mission and Social Concern' offered the following four guidelines:

1. That any programme of social concern must point men to— not away from—the central message of redemption through the blood of Christ.

2. Expression of social concern must provide an opportunity for spoken witness to Christ recognizing the incompleteness of non-verbal witness.

3. Efforts must not arouse unrealistic and unscriptural expectations; the realities of sin and the Second Coming were not to be minimized.

4. The desire to do good in the name of Christ should not lead to wasteful competition with secular agencies.[8]

What can be considered to be a distinctive evangelical approach to social action over and against the more liberal ecumenical approach, continued at the more ambitious Berlin World Congress of Evangelism later that year. The tone and general theological flavour of the conference was captured by the opening address given by Billy Graham in which he firmly maintained that: 'If the church went back to its main task of proclaiming the gospel and getting people converted to Christ, it would have a far greater impact on the social, moral and psychological needs of men than it could achieve through any other thing it could possibly do'.[9]

We find the same outlook echoed at Berlin by John Stott: 'The commission of the Church is not to reform society, but to preach the Gospel. Certainly Christ's disciples who have embraced the Gospel, and who themselves are being transformed by the Gospel, are intended to be salt of the earth and light of the world. That is, they are to influence the society in which they live and work by helping arrest its corruption and illumine its darkness. But the primary task of the members of Christ's Church is to be Gospel heralds, not social reformers.'[10]

As we shall see, Stott was later to move on from this position, but this was the stance taken by the majority of Evangelicals in 1966.

However, it would seem that already at the conference seeds were sown which were later to germinate into an approach to socio-political involvement which would mark a significant change of direction for Evangelicals. As Paul Rees observes: 'If the mission of the Church is narrow, the witness of the believing community is broad. The evangelistic mission is to proclaim "Christ crucified" as the "one mediator" of our salvation. But the confirming witness of believers is one in which they stand related to the whole life and to the total fabric of society. Here they bear witness both to the mercy of God's forgiveness and the judgements of God's justice. Nothing human is alien to their interests and, so far as their testimony and influence are concerned, Jesus Christ is Lord of all.'[11]

The Lausanne Movement

Internationally, the next major development was the Lausanne conference in 1974, which Rachel Tingle claims resulted in a 'paradigm shift' in evangelical thinking.[12] The 'shift' was toward what came to be referred to as 'holistic mission', and the term 'social action' was exchanged for the phrase 'socio-political involvement'. We thus have article 5 of the Lausanne Covenant worded as follows:

'We affirm that God is both the Creator and the Judge of all people. We therefore should share his concern for justice and reconciliation throughout human society and for the liberation of men and women from every kind of oppression. Because men and women are made in the image of God, every person, regardless of race, religion, colour, culture, class, sex or age, has an intrinsic dignity because of which he or she should be respected and served, not exploited. Here too we express penitence both for our neglect and for having sometimes regarded evangelism and social concern as mutually exclusive. Although reconciliation with other people is not reconciliation with God, nor is social action evangelism, nor is political liberation salvation, nevertheless we affirm that evangelism and socio-political involvement are both part of our Christian duty. For both are necessary expressions of our doctrines of God and man, our love for our neighbour and our obedience to Jesus Christ. The message of salvation implies also a message of judgment upon every form of alienation, oppression and discrimination, and we should not be afraid to denounce evil and injustice wherever they exist. When people receive Christ they are born again into his kingdom and must seek not only to exhibit but also to spread its righteousness in the midst of an unrighteous world. The salvation we claim should be transforming us in the totality of our personal and social responsibilities. Faith without works is dead. (Acts 17:26,31; Genesis 18:25; Isaiah 1:17; Psalm 45:7; Genesis 1:26,27; James. 3:9; Leviticus 19:18; Luke 6:27,35; James. 2:14–26; John. 3:3,5; Matthew 5:20; 6:33; II Corinthians 3:18; James. 2:20).'[13]

The statement was in many ways a direct outworking of a paper presented by John Stott at the congress which set the direction for much of what followed. He began by pointing out that in the past 'it was taken for granted that mission and evangelism … were more or less synonymous'.[14] The conclusion of his paper was that biblical evangelism 'is part of God's mission through God's church in God's world.'[15] This came about by redefining mission as 'everything the church is sent into the world to do'[16] as well as proposing that this mission is twofold (arising out of Jesus statement in John 20:21). Thus, 'Mission embraces the church's double vocation to be "the salt of the earth" and "the light of the world." For Christ *sends* the church into the earth to be salt, and *sends* the church into the world to be light.'[17] We shall have cause to question Stott's understanding of these two key phrases in a later chapter, but the logic of his position was clearly set forth.

A year later, John Stott's change in thinking as crystallized at Lausanne was openly admitted, 'Today ... I would express myself differently. It is not just that the commission [i.e. the Great Commission] includes the duty to teach converts everything that Jesus had previously commanded (Matthew 28:20), and that social responsibility is among the things which Jesus commanded. I see now more clearly that not only the consequences of the commission but the actual commission itself must be understood to include social as well as evangelistic responsibility, unless we are to be guilty of distorting the words of Jesus.'[18]

The division, controversy and confusion of the relationship between evangelism and social action continued within the Lausanne movement as illustrated by the following representative statements:[19]

- '... the Gospel is the root, of which both evangelism and social responsibility is the fruit.'

- '... is salvation experienced only by those who consciously confess Jesus Christ as Lord and Saviour? Or is it right in addition to refer to the emergence of justice and peace in the wider community as "salvation" and to attribute to the grace of Christ every beneficial social transformation? Some of us do not find salvation-language inappropriate for such situations, even when Christ is not acknowledged in them. Most of us, however, consider that it is more prudent and biblical to reserve the vocabulary of salvation for the experience of reconciliation with god through Christ and its direct consequences.'

- '... the eschatological vision ... should prove a stimulus to social responsibility. If in heaven they will "hunger no more, neither thirst any more" (Revelation 7:16), should we not feed the hungry today? And if in the end "they shall beat their swords into ploughshares, and their spears into pruning hooks; nation shall not lift up sword against nation, neither shall they learn war anymore" (Micah 4:3; Isaiah 2:4), does that not mean that war is incompatible with the perfect will of God?'

There is little change at Lausanne II (1989) and the Manila manifesto which states: 'Evangelism is primary because our chief concern is with the gospel, that all people may have the opportunity to accept Jesus Christ as Lord and Saviour. Yet Jesus not only proclaimed the Kingdom of God, he also demonstrated its arrival by works of mercy and power. We are called today to a similar integration of words and deeds. In a spirit of humility we are to preach and teach, minister to the sick, feed the hungry, care for prisoners, help the disadvantaged and handicapped, and deliver the oppressed. While we acknowledge the diversity of spiritual gifts, callings and contexts, we also affirm that good news and good works are inseparable.'

There is, however, a slight alteration in language at Lausanne III and the Cape Town Commitment with talk of 'integral mission': 'Integral mission is the proclamation and demonstration of the gospel. It is not simply that evangelism and social involvement are to be done alongside each other. Rather, in integral mission our proclamation has social consequences as we call people to love and repentance in all areas of life. And our social involvement has evangelistic consequences as we bear witness to the transforming grace of Jesus Christ. If we ignore the world, we betray the Word of God which sends us out to serve the world. If we ignore the Word of God, we have nothing to bring to the world.'

One wonders to what extent 'integral mission' is the same as 'holistic mission' but with a different name? In which case there has been a move *back* to the 1900 situation described by Johnston, with evangelism having social consequences which few would deny. But that during recent years evangelicals have tended to move away from the 'balanced' approach of Stott was picked up at the conference by Os Guinness: 'Now all these years later the tendency is almost opposite, because in a globalised world there are many movements on behalf of human rights, justice and the environment and so on. It is easy to be concerned for social justice and many Christians have tended to forget the simple gospel and the part of proclamation again.'[20]

Shifts in Anglican Evangelicalism

Not surprisingly, parallel developments are to be traced within Anglican Evangelicalism as can be observed in the successive National Evangelical Anglican Congresses in 1967, 1977 and 1988. Writing a preparatory paper for NEAC 1 entitled 'Christian Worldliness', Sir Norman Anderson said, 'It has sometimes been debated whether the social teaching of the Bible flows from the doctrines of the person and work of Christ—that is, from the facts of redemption—or not … From my own standpoint, I would simply say that the Bible seems to me to approach questions of social responsibility in terms of the doctrine of creation and of God's plan for the created order, and not primarily in terms of the doctrines of incarnation, redemption and God's plan for His Church …'[21]

However, while the pre-Keele book *Guidelines* reflected much classic evangelical thinking and theology, on the ground prior to the conference changes were afoot.[22] As preparations for the conference were under way, pressure was been brought to bear on John Stott and the organising group to allow for more participation, and it was the 'young Turks' of the day (Philip Crowe, Gavin Reid and Colin Buchanan) who drafted the final statement, which included the following, 'Christians share in God's work of mission by being present among non-Christians to live and to speak for Christ, and in his name to promote justice and meet human need in all its forms. Evangelism and compassionate concern belong together in the mission of God.'[23]

By the time we come to NEAC 3 in 1988 we have one major platform speaker, the then Secretary to the General Synod's Board for

Social Responsibility, John Gladwin, who offered an evangelicalized liberation theology when he said, amongst other things, that 'God broke the back of injustice at the cross'.[24] Also, a leading workshop leader, Dr Chris Sugden stated: 'The content of the Gospel is to be defined in terms of the physically and socially poor.' It would be fair to say that these were representative of a significant number at NEAC 3, such that one observer could write: 'NEAC 3 revealed sharp tensions and unexpected polarisations. Where major platform speakers referred to social or political issues, the style and content of their biblical exegesis and contemporary application engendered heated debate in the chalets and caravans of Caister.'[25]

NEAC 4 in 2003 saw a move back towards a pre-NEAC 2 classic evangelicalism as represented by the main speakers (together with what some would consider a fawning stance towards the Church of England establishment being ensured by the invitation of the then liberal Archbishop of Canterbury, Rowan Williams and the Anglo-Catholic Archbishop of York, David Hope to address the conference).[26] The only high profile reference to social action was in the talk given by Christopher Wright, 'Whose World, Whose Mission?' in which he made a plea for holistic mission.

Broader views in Britain

On the wider evangelical scene many initiatives were taken in Britain to put into practice the purported rediscovered evangelical social conscience. In 1971 the National Festival of Light was launched. O. R. Johnston played a major part in this and was later to take up the position of the chief executive of what was to become the Care Trust's political arm, Care Campaigns. In 1975 he put forward a biblical case for such Christian social involvement at the Leicester Ministers' Conference, later to be published under the title 'Christianity in a Collapsing Culture'. In 1982 the London Institute for Contemporary Christianity (LICC) was founded under the chairmanship of John Stott. This was a creative 'think tank' for Evangelicals wrestling with a wide range of cultural and social matters. Earlier in 1969, the Shaftesbury Project was formed under the umbrella of the Inter-Varsity Fellowship and was later to merge with the LICC to form Christian Impact, now known as the Institute for Contemporary Christianity based at St Peter's, Vere Street in London.

Dr Oliver Barclay summarises what was happening during these years, 'In brief, there was a ferment of thought and activity in the 1970s, which started a good many fresh organisations. The magazine *Third Way* was started in 1977 and, with the IVF's magazine *The Christian Graduate* (later called *Christian Arena*), gave opportunity to discuss these [contemporary issues and matters of social involvement] in a critical way. There was little dispute that it was important to think out a biblical approach to social and political questions.'[27]

There were some serious and troubling theological questions raised by these discussions however,

'Because some warm advocates of social action justified such action on a very flimsy biblical basis. If it was a straightforward attempt to meet social need, because the love of Christ must move us to do something, then there was no problem ... When in this century [20th] social action was advocated on the basis of the doctrine of the kingdom of God, however, it opened up a series of dispute. This was not only because liberal Christians had used this concept to promote unacceptable ideas of a 'social gospel' in the 1930s. Now it was coming in from different sources, especially from the South American writers on 'liberation theology'. Ronald Sider's *Rich Christians in an Age of Hunger* appeared in the USA in 1977 (with an edited version in the UK in 1984) and had considerable impact. He and others following the same line seemed to have been over-influenced by liberation theology, because they argued that all actions of righteousness, even when done by total unbelievers (such as Marxists) were examples of 'kingdom activity' ... The debate unfortunately cast doubt in the minds of some regarding the justification of such activity, if indeed it needed such tenuous theological defence.[28]

Dr Lloyd-Jones and Social Involvement

So far in our brief historical survey one figure has towered above all others, namely, the Anglican, Dr John Stott. However, throughout the changing evangelical landscape in Britain there was another figure which was highly significant, the Free Churchman, Dr Martyn Lloyd-Jones of Westminster Chapel, London. Those familiar with the ministry of Lloyd-Jones will not be surprised to find that on these matters, as on many others, he spoke prophetically.

In the rediscovery of the 'evangelical social conscience' of the 1960s and 70s, appeals were often made to the models set by the great Evangelical Reformers of the nineteenth century. But, as Dr Lloyd-Jones noted, this is a false comparison and doomed to lead to disappointment unless one at the same time recognizes the part played by the eighteenth-century Great Awakening upon such a movement. Of course, herein lies the difference, for we do not live in the aftermath of a Revival! In a letter to Iain Murray concerning the wisdom of publishing an article by Raymond Johnston on Christian social involvement, Lloyd-Jones wrote: 'He [Johnston] completely fails to see that the Wilberforces and the Shaftesburys can only succeed after times of Revival when there are many Christians.'[29]

This does not mean that Dr Lloyd-Jones put all his eggs in the 'Revival basket', as it were, for elsewhere he writes: 'If we give the impression that we have no concern about political and social matters we shall alienate people; and I suggest that we have done so, and so the masses are outside the church. On the other hand, if we think we are going to fill our churches and solve our problems by preaching politics and taking an interest in social matters we are harbouring a very great delusion.'[30]

How, then, are Christians to proceed? In the same address Dr Lloyd-Jones essentially adopts the position of an earlier generation of Evangelicals. 'The New Testament', he argues, presents the Christian as 'salt in society and leaven and surely the whole point of those two comparisons is that Christian influence is to be a quiet influence and a slow process of influencing society'.[31] However, the eschatological dimension must not be minimized: 'The Christian's primary concern must always be the Kingdom of God, and then, because of that the salvation of men's souls.'[32]

With Wesley and Wilberforce we find Dr Lloyd-Jones reiterating, 'Men must be born again. How can they live the

Christian life if they have not become Christians? ... Nevertheless, government and law and order are essential because man is in sin; and the Christian should be the best citizen in the country. The Christian must act as a citizen and play his part in politics and other matters to get the best conditions possible ... and be content with that which is less than Christian ...' [33]

However, 'The Christian must of necessity have a profoundly pessimistic view of life in this world. Man is in sin and therefore you will never produce the perfect society. The coming of Christ alone is going to produce that. The consequence of this pessimism about the preacher's primary duty is to exhort people to be ready to meet their judge.' [34]

Summary

Throughout the 19th and 20th centuries, and indeed into the 21st century, the understanding of the relationship between the Gospel, evangelism and social involvement has been in a state of flux. There are those who see the proclamation of the Gospel as the primary activity of the church in the world which has social entailments. There are others who see social action as primary, as an essential means not only of expressing the Kingdom of God, but as extending it, even by those who do not own the name of Christ, and in some cases are actively opposed to him (Marxists). Still others adopt an integrated approach, both evangelism and social engagement as being equally necessary to the Christian mission. But just how are these positions to be evaluated and what are their ramifications in terms of shaping evangelical theology and practice? These are just some of the questions to which we shall now turn.

ENDNOTES

1. Kathleen Heasman, *Evangelicals in Action: An appraisal of their Social Work in the Victorian Era* (London: Geoffrey Bles, 1962), p. 13

2. Arthur Johnston, *The Battle for World Evangelism*, (Wheaton, Illinois: Tyndale House Publishers, 1978) p. 37

3. Ibid. p. 41

4. Ibid. p. 55

5. Walter Rauschenbusch, *Christianity and the Social Crisis*, (New York: Macmillan, 1907), p. 65

6. Ibid. p. xiii

7. See Efiong S. Utuk 'From Wheaton to Lausanne: The Road to Modification of Contemporary Evangelical Mission Theology' *Missiology: An International Review* 14/2 (1986) pp. 205-20

8. Conference papers published in *The Church's Worldwide Mission,* Harold Lindsell (ed) (Waco, Texas: Word Publishing, 1966)

9. Why The Berlin Congress?' *Christianity Today,* 11 November 1966

10. John Stott, 'The Great Commissions' in *One Race, One Gospel, One Task, World Congress on Evangelism, Berlin, 1966,* Carl. F. Henry and W. Stanley Mooneyham (eds), (World Wide Publications 1967, Vol. 1), pp. 50-1

11. Paul S. Rees 'Evangelism and Social Concern' in Henry and Mooneyham, *One Race, One Gospel, One Task,* Vol. 1, p. 308

12. Rachel Tingle 'Evangelical Social Action Today: Road to Recovery or Road to Ruin?' *The Anglican Evangelical Crisis,* Melvin Tinker (ed) (Fearn, Ross-shire, Christian Focus Publications 1995) p. 196

13. Full text in *'Let the Earth Hear His Voice'* J. D. Douglas (ed) (Minneapolis: World Wide Publications, 1975)

14. John R. W. Stott, 'The Biblical basis for Evangelism', in Douglas, *Let the Earth Hear His Voice,* p. 66

15. Ibid. p. 78

16. Ibid. p. 68

17. Ibid.

18. John R. W. Stott *Christian Mission in the Modern World* (London: Falcon, 1975) p. 23

19. John Woodhouse 'Evangelism and Social Responsibility' B. G. Webb (ed) *Christians in Society* Exploration 3 (Lancer, 1998) p. 18

20. Matthew Cresswell, 'Lausanne's Legacy lacks promise', in *'The Guardian'* newspaper, 29th October, 2010.

21. N. D. Anderson 'Christian Worldliness—the need and limits of Christian involvement' *Guidelines,* J. I. Packer (ed) (CPAS 1967) p. 216

22. Andrew Atherstone, 'The Keele Congress of 1967: A Paradigm Shift in Anglican Evangelical Attitudes.' *Journal of Anglican Studies,* Vol. 9 (2) 175–197, 2011.

23. The Keele Covenant is given in full as Appendix A in C. Yeates (ed.), *'Has Keele Failed?'* (Hodder and Stoughton, 1995).

24. See Melvin Tinker, 'NEAC 3—A Conference Too Far? *Churchman* 1988 Vol. 102

25. Vera Sinton 'Evangelical Social Ethics: Has it Betrayed the Gospel?'

in Melvin Tinker (ed.) *Restoring the Vision* (Oxford: Monarch, 1990) p. 130

26. See, Melvin Tinker, 'NEAC 4 and Rowan Williams', www.e-n.org. uk/2003/07/features/archbishop-rowan-williams-and-neac-4/

27. O. R. Barclay, *Evangelicalism in Britain 1935-1995* (Leicester: IVP, 1997), p. 109

28. Ibid. pp. 109-110

29. *Dr Martyn Lloyd-Jones Letters 1919–1981* (Edinburgh: Banner of Truth 1994) p. 222

30. Dr Martyn Lloyd-Jones 'The Christian and the State in Revolutionary Times', *The Puritans Their Origins and Successors* (Edinburgh: Banner of Truth, 1987) pp 342-43

31. Ibid. p. 341

32. Ibid. 'The Christian and the State' p. 343

33. Ibid. p. 344

34. Ibid. p. 345

2

How is history to be read?

Dr John Woodhouse notes that 'a different understanding of our present situation produces a different understanding of where we have come from. The point is clear: history looks different depending upon your vantage point.'[1]

Having given a brief, potted history of evangelicals and social involvement in the 20th and early 21st century, we shall then consider how these matters might be evaluated.

The Great Reversal

There is no question of the significance of evangelical social involvement in the 19th century.[2] But this changed, as already noted, in the earlier part of the 20th century as evangelicals became less concerned about social issues and as a consequence, less involved. The change has been referred to as 'The Great Reversal', a term initially coined by the American historian Timothy L. Smith and then popularized by the sociologist David Moberg in a book which incorporates the phrase in its title.[3]

Moberg notes the following influences which accounts for this evangelical withdrawal:[4]

1. The disillusion brought by the Great War to those who had believed in the inevitable progress of humankind aided by the development of science and technology. This began to be replaced with a greater pessimism about the possibility of removing evil from society and establishing God's kingdom.

2. The fundamentalist-modernist controversy. As this developed there was an increased identification of Christian attempts to influence legislation and basic social structures with the Social Gospel movement. Subsequently the various parties involved began to polarise. The Social Gospellers gave more attention to social evils whilst the fundamentalists placed greater emphasis on personal sin and the need for personal repentance and salvation. Putting it crudely, the former emphasised the corporate dimensions of sin, the latter, the individual dimension. 'Christians became either evangelistically or socially involved but not both.'[5]

3. Millennialism. This was the era of a strong belief in the idea of progress. This was especially so in the United States where postmillennialists in the Social Gospel movement argued that the golden age was just around the corner. D.L. Moody took this to be rank heresy. For him and many others, the world was a ruined vessel and Christians were exhorted to set their sights on heaven. Premillennialism took an entirely different view to the postmillennialists, namely, that social conditions would inevitably worsen until the return of Christ. A consequence was that many evangelicals of the premillennialist stripe became more detached from social involvement.

4. The overwhelming complexity and enormity of the problems of urbanisation and industrialisation led some evangelicals to the conclusion that there really was little else that they could do to alleviate much of the human misery caused by such developments other than pray and evangelise. The question of hermeneutics is also thrown into the mix for since the Bible did not directly address many of these modern issues, some thought they could not be addressed *at all* from a Biblical standpoint.

There then followed several decades when evangelicals lacked the sense of social responsibility of their 19th century forbears, 'Unlike them, modern evangelicals tend to be politically and socially conservative and right wing, strong on personal morality but reactionary on social issues, committed to evangelism but not committed to helping the poor and needy of society now. On the other side of the fence, this has been the period in which "liberation theology" has taken shape, calling, in some of its proponents, for a moratorium on preaching and a new emphasis on changing the structures of society.'[6]

The Great Rediscovery

The 'Great Reversal' has been seen by some as being replaced by the 'Great Rediscovery', a view proposed by John Stott in 1984, 'One of the most notable features of the world-wide evangelical movement during the last ten to fifteen years has been the recovery of our temporarily mislaid social conscience. For approximately fifty years (c 1920–1970) evangelicals were preoccupied with the task of defending the historical biblical faith against the attacks of liberalism, and reacting against its "social gospel". But we are convinced that God has given us social as well as evangelistic responsibilities in his world. Yet the half-century of neglect has put us far behind in this area. We have a long way to catch up.'[7]

As we have seen, Stott had been in the forefront ensuring that the much needed 'catching up' actually took place. Dr Stott had been at pains to stress that the consultation at Lausanne I endorsed the primacy of evangelism, a priority underscored at Lausanne II at Manila in 1989:

> Evangelism is primary because our chief concern is with the gospel, that all people may have the opportunity to accept Jesus Christ as their Lord and Saviour. The Grand Rapids Consultation of 1982 sought to tease out the relationship between evangelism and social responsibility in the following way: First, social activity is a consequence of the Gospel, so 'faith works through love'. But, the report goes on to say 'social responsibility is more than a consequence of evangelism; it is one of its principal aims'. Secondly, 'social activity is a bridge to evangelism'. And thirdly, 'social activity … accompanies [evangelism] as its partner. They are like the two blades of a pair of scissors or the two wings of a bird, as they were in the public ministry of Jesus.' The partnership is, in reality, a marriage.[8]

From a Free Church background, Derek Tidball offers a similar assessment, namely, that as far as social action was concerned, 'evangelicals betrayed their heritage' but now are 'on the road to recovery'.[9]

A corroboration of this view has also been expressed by Nigel Biggar, 'In the early 1970s evangelical interest in social ethics was reawakened. After at least two generations of neglect, partly attributable to a reaction against the substitution of social reform for religious conversion by the social gospel movement, the political unrest of the late 1960s provoked evangelicals on both sides of the Atlantic to ask themselves how Christian faith could respond to the burning questions of the day.' [10]

Biggar sees this as being nothing less than a returning to the stance of the 19th century Evangelicals of Great Britain, 'To a certain extent, they were thereby resuming the social concern of some of their nineteenth century forbears. Some of these, most famously William Wilberforce and Anthony Ashley Cooper, the 7th Earl of Shaftesbury, had been deeply distressed by certain social ills of the time and campaigned tirelessly for their alleviation.' But, as we shall see in a later chapter, there has been a significant departure from the Victorian Evangelicals, as Biggar himself acknowledges. [11]

The Great Betrayal

Others have a less sanguine view of the more recent turn of events. Nigel Biggar sees the 'Great Reversal' as a 'betrayal of the evangelical heritage', others would see what is being presented as the 'Great Rediscovery' as in fact the 'Great Betrayal'.

Arthur Johnston has undertaken two substantial surveys of developments amongst evangelicals in relation to evangelism and social engagement and has expressed deep concern that far from recovering their heritage, evangelicals are in serious danger of losing it. [12]

That concern is articulated by Peter Beyerhaus in his preface to Johnston's, *The Battle for World Evangelism:* 'It is particularly one new element, widely hailed by others as a sign that the new Evangelicals have come of age, about which I—like my friend Arthur Johnston—have argued with my other beloved friend John Stott. For, unlike some of our Latin American colleagues I consider this element incompatible with the concept of evangelism as normatively expounded by both the Fathers of the Reformation and of the Evangelical Awakening. I am referring to the theological co-ordination of evangelism and socio-political involvement as equally constitutive elements of our Christian duty, or even—which is not the same—of the mission which Christ gave to His Church.'[13]

Johnston is of the view that it was principally at Lausanne that the theology of evangelism became blunted because it lost the unique status it had previously held in evangelical thinking prior to Berlin 1966.[14] In contrast to Stott's upbeat assessment of what happened in evangelicalism in the 1970s and 80s we have this statement by Johnston, 'This century has experienced a decline of evangelism associated with the modernism and liberalism introduced into Western Christianity during the nineteenth century.'[15]

Others who would identify with the call for Evangelicals to engage in social involvement have expressed similar concerns. Thus Sir Fred Catherwood comments: 'In the sixties I wrote that we evangelicals should come out of our pietistic ghetto and take part in the social debate as Christian citizens ... I and others in the movement won the argument. But we also lost a vital part of the case we were making. We did not allow for the "zeitgeist". We argued that it was the task of the Christian church to bring the trends in public opinion to the standards of eternal truth and judge them by God's word. But that was not what happened. The evangelicals joined the liberals in a concern for social issues, but it was the world and not the church which set the agenda.'[16]

We find echoes of the same concern in Rachel Tingle's survey, 'From what we have seen, then, in this brief overview of immensely complex processes, the renewed concern for evangelical social action we are seeing in Britain today is only partly a return to the nineteenth century heritage. It is also partly a return to the old social gospel, recycled via the ecumenical movement and liberation theology, and now adopted with only minor modifications by a radical strand of evangelicalism. Because of this a divide has been opening up within world evangelicalism which over the past thirty years has been getting ever wider. Anglican evangelicals in Britain find themselves on both sides of this divide which the Anglo-Catholic theologian, Kenneth Leech, has referred to as a "new reformation". As he says, "increasingly the real division within world Christianity does not run along historic denominational lines. It is a division between those who believe that the Kingdom of God involves the transformation of the world and its structures of injustice, and those who do not". He might equally well have said that it is a division between those who see the gospel primarily in socio-political terms and those who do not. For this debate is only superficially about social action. It is fundamentally about the meaning of the gospel of Christ.' [17]

How great that division is might be gauged by comparing the Reforming Evangelicals of the 19th century with the Radical Evangelicals of the 20th and 21st centuries. It is to this comparison that we now turn.

ENDNOTES

1. John Woodhouse, 'Evangelism and Social responsibility' in B. G. Webb (ed), *Christians in Society*, (Explorations 3, Lancer, 1988), p. 9

2. See, J. Wesley Bready, *England Before and After Wesley* (London: Hodder & Stoughton, 1939)

3. David O. Moberg, *The Great Reversal: Evangelism and Social Action* (J. B. Lippincott Company, 1977)

4. See Woodhouse, op cit., pp. 6-7

5. David O. Moberg, op cit., pp. 77-81

6. Woodhouse, op cit., p. 7

7. John R. W. Stott, *Issues facing Christians Today*, (Basingstoke: Marshall Pickering, 1984) p. xi

8. John R. W. Stott 'Holistic Mission', *The Contemporary Christian* (Leicester: IVP, 1992) p. 340.

9. Derek Tidball, *Who are the Evangelicals?*, (London: Marshall Pickering, 1994), pp. 188, 194.

10. Nigel Biggar, 'Evangelism and Social Ethics', in *Evangelical Anglicans, Their Role and Influence in the Church Today* (eds. R. T. France and A. E. McGrath, SCM, 1993), p. 108.

11. Ibid. p. 108

12. Arthur P. Johnston, *World Evangelism and the Word of God* (Minneapolis: Bethany Fellowship 1974) and *The Battle for World Evangelism* (Wheaton, Illinois: Tyndale House, 1978).

13. Johnston, *The Battle for World Evangelism* p. 10.

14. Johnston, *The Battle for World Evangelism*, pp. 329-30.

15. Ibid. p. 23.
16. Sir Fred Catherwood 'The Zeitgeist' *Transformation*, October/ December 1986
17. Rachel Tingle, op cit., pp 201- 202.

3

Reformers and Radicals

What is the continuity and discontinuity between what some of
the great eighteenth and nineteenth-century evangelical social
Reformers taught about their theological and moral motivation
and the heirs of Lausanne?

The Reforming Evangelicals

The social reforms of the nineteenth century took place in the
wake of the revivals of the eighteenth century which provided
the moral context and spiritual impetus for the reforms. The
relationship between the two has been carefully considered by J
Wesley Bready in his engrossing, *'England Before and After Wesley'*.
What did Wesley teach about the gospel and social action? In his
Preface to the first Methodist Hymn Book (1739) Wesley wrote,
'The Gospel of Christ knows no religion but social, no holiness but
social holiness. This command have we from Christ, that he who
loves God loves his brother also.'

In the University sermon delivered in St Mary's, Oxford in
1774, Wesley pictured Christianity as 'Beginning to exist in
individuals', next as 'spreading from one to another', and finally
'as covering the earth'. He then asked his congregation to pause
'and survey this strange sight—a Christian world!' He proceeded
to challenge those in leadership positions within the town as to
whether they were of one mind with the love of God shed abroad
in their hearts (i.e. converted). He then pleaded that the sure hope
for a better age was a better man and only Christ's new man can

herald Christ's new world. So Henry Carter comments: 'To Wesley a scheme of reconstructing society which ignored the redemption of the individual was unthinkable.'[1]

Similarly, Bready writes of Wesley, 'As a prophet of God and an ordained ambassador of Christ, he did not conceive it his task to formulate economic, political and social theories; nor did he judge himself competent so to do. His 'calling' he believed was far more sacred, and more thoroughgoing: it was to lead men into contact with spiritual reality, to enable them to possess their souls and enter the realms of abundant life. For if once men, in sufficient numbers, were endowed with an illumined conscience and spiritual insight they, collectively as well as individually, would become possessors of the 'wisdom that passeth knowledge'; and in that wisdom social problems gradually would be solved.'[2]

Wesley saw his priority as preaching the gospel. Being a Christian also entailed good works, being a good citizen, indeed, being a good neighbour. The Christian was committed to the second great commandment: 'Love your neighbour as yourself.' But Wesley saw that the first commandment held pride of place, 'Hear, O Israel: The Lord our God, the Lord is one. And you shall love the Lord your God with all your heart and with all your soul and with all your mind and with all your strength.' (Mark 12:29–31). How can men and women love God while they are in enmity with him? How can people be addressed as 'Israel' unless they belong to 'Israel'? Reconciliation is first required and the means of that reconciliation is the gospel.

As Bready demonstrates, Wesley's impressive endeavours in promoting social action, working towards slavery abolition, ameliorating the effects of gambling and liquor abuse, promoting literacy and education amongst the poor, as well as his more conspicuous political comments regarding the American Revolution, arose from a Spirit-fired application of the following fundamental Christian doctrines: (1) Our unity and responsibilities as creatures before the Creator, (2) The corruption of the will by sin, so that all social problems are fundamentally spiritual, (3) The principle of stewardship and the future judgement to come. At no point did Wesley conceive social action as possessing the same theological weight or primacy as Gospel proclamation, although the latter entailed the former.

When we turn to William Wilberforce we find the same principles at work.

Wilberforce is most widely known for his part in the abolition of the slave trade, but he also had another great aim. On Sunday, 28th of October, 1787 he wrote in his diary: 'God Almighty has set before me two great objects, the suppression of the Slave Trade and the Reformation of Manners', that is, a new Society with a view to raising the moral tone of the nation by clamping down on offences such as the publication of indecent or blasphemous literature and the desecration of the Lord's Day. Jonathan Bayes in his treatment of this campaign notes: 'His plan was that his Society for the Reformation of Manners should serve to restore England to its Protestant faith by standing against those moral offences which militated against Christianity. As a by-product, Wilberforce believed, there would follow a general moral improvement.'[3]

Being the shrewd politician that he was, Wilberforce did not restrict the membership of the society to Evangelicals. Initially he couched his campaign in purely moral terms. But then he went further to challenge the religious outlook of many by writing his book, 'A Practical View of the Prevailing Religious System of Professed Christians in the Higher and Middle Classes in this Country Contrasted with Real Christianity.' This was published in 1797, having taken four years to write. Wilberforce's aim was to share his testimony and to lead members of his own class into vital Christianity by exposing the shallowness of nominal Christianity. The book, much to the surprise of the printer, went through five reprints within six months and just kept on selling!

Wilberforce argued that the general lack of concern with true Christianity could be traced back to two maxims: 'One is that it signifies little what a man believes; look to his practice. The other (of the same family) is that sincerity is all in all.' So he writes: 'The first of these maxims proceeds from the monstrous supposition that, although we are accountable creatures, we shall not be called upon to account before God for the exercise of our intellectual ... powers. The second ... proceeds on this groundless supposition:

The Supreme Being has not afforded us sufficient means of discriminating truth from falsehood or right from wrong.'

The ignorance of basic Christian truths was the result, argued Wilberforce, of a failure to recognize the depth and extent of man's moral depravity through original sin and that although nominal religion may pay lip service to Christ, it lacked that which was required of authentic faith, a commitment of the totality of one's life so that everything is done to the glory of God.

Bayes suggests that in the medium and long term, the impact of both the Society and 'A Practical View' was considerable. He contends that the improved moral mood in society in the 1830s and the sense of being accountable to God which pervaded society at every level was, 'in no small measure due to Wilberforce'. However, as 'A Practical View' shows, Wilberforce, like Wesley before him, saw conversion as being the main need, especially given his strong view of human corruption by original sin. In drawing out some of the implications for today, Bayes concludes: 'Like Wilberforce we need to be convinced of the primacy of conversion: until men and women are made new by the Holy Spirit, there will never be a genuine external reformation.' [4]

Of particular significance in shaping the Reforming Evangelicals' approach to social involvement was their view of eschatology and the reality of the judgement to come. For example, Anthony Ashley-Cooper, the Earl of Shaftesbury, confessed: 'I do not think in the last forty years I have lived one conscious hour that was not influenced by the thought of our Lord's return.' Wilberforce in his 'A Practical View' writes of the authentic believer: 'That he was created by God, redeemed from death, the consequence of original sin, by the incarnation of the Son of God, who had commanded him to be grateful and pious towards God, merciful and benevolent towards men; ... and that, as he neglected or obeyed these commands, he was to expect punishment or reward in a future life.'

Such an understanding of the relation between gospel renewal and societal reformation is very similar to the position advocated at Wheaton and Berlin in 1966 but rests less easily with what some Evangelicals have proposed since.

The model of the Reforming Evangelicals might be contrasted with that of the Radical Evangelicals whose spiritual pedigree, as we shall argue, can be traced directly back to Lausanne.[5]

The Radical Evangelicals

Nigel Biggar rightly observes that as well as the present evangelical interest in social problems comprising a resumption of an earlier tradition of concern, it also represents a new departure. What marks the point of departure? 'For contemporary evangelicals are much more inclined than their Victorian predecessors to conceive of economic and social life as the proper objects of divine redemption—as indicated by their appeal to the incarnation as the basis of Christian social involvement, and by their emphasis on the social nature of the Kingdom of God.'[6]

Ranald Macaulay observes that at Lausanne a rift occurred which centred on the meaning of the phrase 'Kingdom of God'.[7] This is key to understanding much of the debate that has ensued.

Back in 1967, in his paper for NEAC 1, Sir Norman Anderson argued: 'There is a sense in which that Kingdom is already a present reality, for the King is already on his throne, waiting till all things are put under his feet ... But is there a wider sense in which one can think of the Kingdom as advanced wherever the will of the King is done, even by those who do not give Him personal allegiance? This, it seems to me, is dangerous ground, for we cannot regard the Kingdom of God as having materialized in a factory for example, merely because social justice and harmony reign therein ... The Evangelical holds no brief for the so-called "social gospel", for society, as such, cannot be "redeemed" or "baptised into Christ"... But it can be reformed.'[8]

Matters have moved on a long way since then, for the Radical Evangelical would contest almost everything in Anderson's statement. Rather ironically, in the first Sir Norman Anderson lecture delivered at the Salt and Light Conference at Swanwick, 1998, we find Graham Cray stating: 'Jesus' proclamation concerned the "reign of God"—God who is creator, upholder and consummator of all that is. We are not talking about one sector of human affairs ... we are talking about the reign and sovereignty of God over all that is.' Then in an attempt to substantiate the belief that the Kingdom of God is extended by the Spirit via non-Christians he said: 'Since Pentecost the Spirit has been poured out on all flesh, not just all Christians.' The same argument has been advanced by former Principal of Spurgeon's College, Dr Nigel Wright: 'All the earth is the Lord's and so we trace the Spirit at work beyond the Church, especially in movements that make for human dignity and liberation.'[9]

Dr Chris Sugden, also advocating the Kingdom of God as the basis for evangelical socio-political involvement, extends the redeeming work of Christ on the Cross to cover all positive social change in society: 'Jesus' rule and action are cosmic. He disarmed the principalities and powers which create division in society. Where we see barriers broken down, can we divorce this from God's will seen in Christ's victory over the powers on the cross? (e.g. between Jew and Gentile slave and free (Galatians 3:28))' and 'this understanding gives us a basis for seeing God at work in society beyond the church applying the effects of Christ's victory on the cross through social change.'[10]

Developing this point, Sugden and Samuel argue that any movement, Christian or not, which tries to establish social justice is to be interpreted as having the same character as Jesus' Kingdom acts of power and healing.[11]

What are we to make of such a claim?

First of all, it is based upon a dubious understanding of the term 'Kingdom of God' which means far more than 'God rules'. In Scripture it is something to be entered into, sought, requiring poverty of spirit (Matthew 5:3; 7:21; 7:13). As Professor D. A. Carson correctly maintains, it is to be understood in terms of the sphere of salvation entered into through faith in Jesus Christ.[12]

R. T. France similarly contends: 'It is wrong to identify the Kingdom of God with social reform as it is with the church or heaven, and for the same reason: it is a category mistake ... To talk of men, even Christian men, bringing about God's kingdom is to usurp God's sovereignty. Yet this sort of language is increasingly being heard in evangelical circles. It is strangely reminiscent of the language of 19th century liberalism, which called upon men to create a just and caring society which was called the "Kingdom of God".' [13]

Secondly, Scripture is being handled in a way which is hermeneutically suspect from an evangelical point of view. Instead of Scripture being determinative, it is the *context* in which the Christian finds himself which shapes belief and biblical interpretation. In the NEAC 3 booklet, *Evangelical Roots,* Chris Sugden states: 'The Good News we love is defined in the Scripture as good news to the (physically and socially) poor; and that means that what the good news means to poor Christians (in Scripture and today) should set the criteria for focusing what the good news means to others.' [14]

Elsewhere Dr Sugden gives an example of how this contextualized exegesis works out in practice with a group of Christians operating amongst quarry workers in Bangalore. The team sought to 'affirm' the socially oppressed workers' desire for security 'in the light of the Bible'. Therefore, it is asked: 'Had not God provided Israel with land, a place to belong and access to resources?' So they began to work with the quarry workers towards their goal. A pay rise resulted and the workers attributed their good fortune to God. 'This' it is claimed by Sugden, 'represented the starting-point for these people to enter the life of the Kingdom'. [15]

Not only is this 'paradigmatic approach' to interpreting Scripture common to the proponents of liberation theology, it is reminiscent of the principles taught by the peddlers of prosperity healing. But we might ask: why select these themes of Exodus and Blessing? Why not the prophetic call of Jeremiah that the oppressed people of God should not rebel against the tyrant Nebuchadnezzar?

Also, when it is said by Dr Sugden that wherever 'just relationships are established we are to take these signs of God's Kingdom', and Galatians 3:28 is cited in support, it must be firmly pointed out that what Paul is referring to is what happens in the *church* as a result of people hearing the gospel, and not 'just relationships' in society at large.

Such a loose and selective approach to handling the Bible hardly accords with what is generally regarded as a hallmark of Evangelicalism, namely, respecting the historical integrity of the text and how it functions within the overall canonical sweep of Scripture.

Thirdly, it is worth noting that the Kingdom approach of the Radical Evangelicals to social ethics is remarkably similar to that of Rauschenbusch, as Brian Stanley observes: 'This is extremely difficult to distinguish from the claim of Rauschenbusch that wherever corporations abandon monopoly capitalism for the "law of service" or undemocratic nations submit to real democracy "therewith they step out of the Kingdom of Evil into the Kingdom of God".'[16]

It is evident that it bears little, if any, relation to the Reforming Evangelicals of the eighteenth and nineteenth centuries. So Oliver Barclay comments: 'I can discover no signs of Kingdom thinking in the programmes of Wilberforce, the "Clapham Sect" and Shaftesbury ... They ... used much more straightforward biblical themes.'[17]

Elsewhere Dr Barclay writes: 'Certainly we seem to be doing much less than our theologically less sophisticated nineteenth-century forebears did. There is no evidence that the nineteenth-century evangelicals were troubled by these theological questions. They accepted a straightforward responsibility to help the deprived, and therefore set to work to tackle some of the structures that upheld such deprivation.'[18]

If this is the case, it is indeed a sad indictment on British evangelicals.

The slide away from the Gospel into confusing social involvement with the Gospel itself is illustrated more recently by the book, *The Hole in Our Gospel: What Does God Expect of Us?*[19] This is a survey of worldwide poverty leading its author, Richard Stearns, to conclude that the failure to take up God's mandate to deal with such poverty is 'the hole in our Gospel.'

With regards to this book, D. A. Carson makes three observations.[20]

'First, "what God expects of us" (his subtitle) is, by definition, not the gospel. This is not the great news of what God has done for us in Christ Jesus. Had Mr Stearns cast his treatment of poverty as one of the things to be addressed by the second greatest commandment, or as one of several entailments of the gospel, I could have recommended his book with much greater confidence. As it is, the book will contribute to declining clarity as to what the gospel is.'

'Second, even while acknowledging—indeed, insisting on the importance of genuine needs that Mr Stearns depicts in his book, it is disturbing not to hear similar anguish over human alienation from God. The focus of his book is so narrowly poverty, that the sweep of what the gospel addresses is lost to view. Men and women stand under God's judgment, and this God of love mandates that by the means of heralding the gospel they will be saved not only in this life but in the life to come. Where is the anguish that contemplates a Christ-less eternity, that cries, "Repent! Turn away from all your offenses … Why will you die, people of Israel? For I take no pleasure in the death of anyone" (Ezekiel 18:30–32). The analysis of the problem is too small, and the gospel is correspondingly reduced.'

'Third, some studies have shown that Christians spend about five times more mission dollars on issues related to poverty than they do on evangelism and church planting. At one time, "holistic ministry" was an expression intended to move Christians beyond proclamation to include deeds of mercy. Increasingly, however, "holistic ministry" refers to deeds of mercy without any proclamation of the gospel—and that is not holistic. It is not even halfistic, since the deeds of mercy are not the gospel: they are entailments of the gospel. Although I know many Christians who happily combine fidelity to the gospel, evangelism, church planting, and energetic service to the needy, and although I know some who call themselves Christians who formally espouse the gospel but who live out few of its entailments, I also know Christians who, in the name of a "holistic" gospel, focus all their energy on presence, wells in the Sahel, fighting disease, and distributing food to the poor, but who never, or only very rarely, articulate the gospel, preach the gospel, announce the gospel, to anyone. Judging by the distribution of American mission dollars, the biggest hole in our gospel is the gospel itself.'

Much of what Carson says about Stearns' book in particular can well be applied to the 'radical evangelicalism' in general. This review alone puts paid to the claim referred to in the introduction to this book by Jonathan Chaplin, that scholars have made a 'compelling case' that the Gospel of Jesus 'thrusts us out into the world to be servants of healing, justice and peace' and that the debates regarding the priority of evangelism over social action are 'tired'.

Consistency or corruption?

It may be argued, however, that the departure of the Radical Evangelicals from the evangelical mainstream is an aberration and not a necessary result of the changes which took place at Lausanne I and II. After all, Stott himself would hardly have endorsed the 'Kingdom' approach outlined above. In fact, in his response to another 'Kingdom' advocate, Ron Sider, he is so critical that he can write: 'I still want to insist that the kingdom of God in the New Testament is fundamentally a Christological concept and that it may be said to exist only where Jesus Christ is consciously acknowledged as Lord.'[21]

But it may well be the case that the Radical Evangelicals were simply attempting to be consistent in drawing out the implications of the way of thinking that was developing at these conferences. The result is the emergence of two streams of thought: those represented by the likes of Catherwood and Anderson who would be placed in the Reforming Evangelical category, and those represented by Sugden and Wright who would be identified with Radical Evangelicalism and its salient similarities with the old liberalism. If this is so, then the position of Dr Stott is most interesting, for it would appear that there is an internal inconsistency in his position which places him with a foot in both camps.

Therefore, going back to Dr Stott's treatment of the results of the Grand Rapids Consultation, it may be granted that while the Reforming Evangelicals would have agreed that 'social activity is a consequence of evangelism', one would be hard pressed to find any evidence that they would have shared the view that it was one of its 'principle aims'. Where in the New Testament is this ever put forward as being the case if evangelism is taken as proclaiming the evangel? The evangel as presented by the apostle Paul in his letter to the Romans displays no indication of social transformation being integral to the message; rather, it is a spiritual transformation which is its focus. As people's relationship with God is changed, social change also takes place, which is primarily, although not exclusively, within the realm of the redeemed community—the church: Ephesians 1:13: 'And you also became God's people when you heard the true message, the Good News that brought you salvation. You believed in Christ, and God put his stamp of ownership on you by giving you the Holy Spirit he promised' (GNB).

Some, like Paul Schrotenboer, however, would question this definition of the evangel: 'I would see the term "holistic evangelism" as including both the telling of the Good News and the regal summons to convert to God and the call for social systemic reform in the name of Christ.' [22] But this is a tactical move, establishing a definition *a priori* which outmanoeuvres and displaces all others. Schrotenboer may define evangelism in this way, but does the Bible? The answer is surely 'No'.

Was Paul's aim as an evangelist to bring about social change? Not directly. His priestly duty of proclaiming the gospel of God was 'so that the offering of the Gentiles may be acceptable, sanctified by the Holy Spirit' (Romans 15:16). That is, they become incorporated into the people of God by believing the message of repentance and forgiveness of sins through the Lord Jesus Christ.

But if social responsibility is put forward as a principle *aim* in evangelism, it is a small and logical step to conceiving social change as part of the evangel itself. To take that step is to produce 'another Gospel'

ENDNOTES

1. Cited in J. Wesley Bready, *England Before and After Wesley* (London: Hodder & Stoughton, 1939), p. 203

2. Ibid. p. 257

3. Jonathan Bayes 'William Wilberforce—His Impact on Nineteenth Century Society' *Churchman* Vol 2, 1994 p. 125

4. Ibid. p. 134

5. For an exposition of what this term means and entails, see Nigel Wright *The Radical Evangelical*, (London: SPCK 1996)

6. Biggar, op cit., p. 108.

7. Ranald Macaulay 'The Great Commissions' *Cambridge Papers* Vol. 7, no 2 1998

8. Anderson, 'Christian Worldliness' *Guidelines* p. 231

9. Wright op cit., p112

10. Chris Sugden *Kingdom and Creation in Social Ethics* (Grove Ethical Studies No 79, Sugden and Barclay, 1990) p. 20

11. See Vinay Samuel and Chris Sugden 'God's Intention of the World; Tensions Between Eschatology and History' in Tom Sine (ed.) *The Church in Response to Human Need* (Grand Rapids: Eerdmans, 1987) pp. 225-6

12. D. A. Carson, *The Sermon on the Mount: An Evangelical Exposition of Matthew 5-7* (Grand Rapids, MI: Baker Book House, 1982) pp 225-6

13. R. T. France 'The Church and The Kingdom of God' D. A. Carson (ed) *Biblical Interpretation and the Church—Text and Context* (Exeter: Paternoster Press, 1984) p. 41

14. Chris Sugden 'Passage to India' in *Evangelical Roots* (Church of England Evangelical Council: 1988) p. 27

15. Op cit. p. 27

16. B. Stanley 'Evangelical Social and Political Ethics: An Historical Perspective' *Evangelical Quarterly* 62: 1(1990) pp 19-26

17. Barclay *'Kingdom and Creation in Social Ethics'* (Grove, 1990) p. 23

18. O. R. Barclay *Evangelicalism In Britain, 1935-1995, a Personal Sketch* (Leicester: IVP, 1997) p. 111

19. Richard Stearn, *The Hole in Our Gospel: What Does God Expect of Us?* (Nashville: Nelson, 2009)

20. D. A. Carson, 'The Hole in Our Gospel', *Themelios,* Vol 38, Issue, 3 (2013)

21. R. J. Sider, with a Response from J. W. Stott, *Evangelism, Salvation and Social Action* (Nottingham: Grove Books, 1977)

22. Paul G. Schrotenboer 'Response to the Article by Lesslie Newbigin' *International Bulletin of Missionary Research* 6/4 (1982) p. 152

4

Tim Keller and Mercy Ministries

A Model for co-ordinating Evangelism
and Social Involvement?

Both Dr John Stott and Dr Martyn Lloyd-Jones were two of
the outstanding evangelical leaders of the post-war generation
in the West in general and Britain in particular. As we have
seen, their views on the relation between evangelism and social
involvement were significant in influencing that generation from
a classic evangelical standpoint in different directions. One of the
significant evangelical leaders of a later generation is Dr Timothy
Keller of Redeemer Presbyterian Church, New York who has
sought both in teaching and practice to co-ordinate evangelism
and social action in terms of what is called 'Ministries of Mercy'.[1]

Since Dr Keller's seminal book was first published nearly twenty
years ago, Redeemer Presbyterian Church has implemented to an
impressive degree many of the ideas presented in the book for
'mercy ministries'. What Keller says of the Bible's concern for
the poor constitutes a real challenge to many evangelicals living
in the West today. Simply as a matter of demonstrating love of
neighbour, churches could and should devise ministries of mercy
appropriate to their situation. The chapters on the character of
mercy, motivation, giving and keeping, and the church and world
are profoundly insightful, containing much which evangelicals
need to hear, consider and practice.

However, where Keller appears to be weak is in the theological justification given for such ministries and the way in which he attempts to co-ordinate evangelism and social action. Central to his argument is the parable of the Good Samaritan which forms the basis for the book's subtitle and main thrust of his thesis— 'The Call of the Jericho Road.' Put simply, the contention is that the story of the Good Samaritan cannot sustain the theological weight Keller tries to place upon it. However, we shall see that it does have a significant role to play, but one which is much simpler but no less penetrating than that suggested by Dr Keller.

This chapter has a twofold focus. First, to offer a constructive critique of the way Keller uses this parable as a basis for social action and how he attempts to co-ordinate this with the task of evangelism. The danger in doing this, of course, is that we end up finding ourselves falling into the trap of the lawyer in Luke's narrative who seeks to 'justify himself' and so excuse himself from acts of mercy. And so secondly, we shall reexamine the parable afresh using rhetorical and cultural analysis in order to see what, if any, are some of the implications for social action by churches today.[2]

Ministries of Mercy and the Jericho Road

Tim Keller claims that *whoever* is in need is our neighbour: 'Someone once said that a "World Christian" needs to read the newspaper along with the Bible. In a sense, this parable of Jesus *directs* us to do so. Though the law expert sought to limit the concept of "neighbour," Jesus expands the concept by showing that *anyone* in need is our neighbour.'[3] Both the story in Luke 10 and the references made to Deuteronomy 15:7ff[4] would indicate that it is not as simple as that, any more than is the claim that we are 'all living on the Jericho Road.'[5] It is probably morally significant that the Samaritan was a neighbour to someone who was in need which *he came across*. This brings into play the principle of 'moral distance'. Was the Samaritan to take responsibility for caring for *all* those who were mugged on the Jericho road and so setting up a ministry of mercy on a permanent basis? That would be the *reductio ad absurdum* of what Dr Keller is arguing. Rather, the Samaritan *was* responsible for the person in need who lay in his path. The fault of the Levite and Priest was that in seeing the need they passed by on the other side. Keller seems to treat the whole world as our 'Jericho Road'. This is where the notion of moral distance comes into play.

No individual or group of individuals can take on responsibility for all needs in a 'Jericho Road' world (or city)—a moral distance exists which reduces personal and corporate responsibility. However, following the principle of Deuteronomy 15:7 ff, if we are *faced* with people in need (whoever they are) then we are under a moral obligation to respond to their need according to the resources we have at our disposal, (the Samaritan used his wine, oil, mule and money—he could not have been held to account for using what he did *not* have—for example, ointment which was not in his pack). Thus, 'our neighbour' is *not*, as Keller claims, 'anyone in need'; it is anyone in need with *whom we have to do.* The Samaritan's neighbours were not everyone else who happened to travel that road at that time or any other, but the person lying *before* him in need. Of course others because of their position and influence might have other moral responsibilities to carry out—for example, a Jericho police chief would have responsibility to make the Road a safer place on which to travel. But the point remains that there are limits to moral responsibility, but because of the wickedness of the human heart and our innate desire to 'justify ourselves' we need to be very careful in examining our motives before claiming what these might be. The other side of the coin is because of a sensitive conscience and desire to please God we are made to feel guilty about not helping people, a guilt which is sometimes unwarranted.

The key chapter to Keller's theological understanding of the relationship between evangelism and social action is chapter 7. He states in his overview, 'The ministry of mercy is not just a means to the end of evangelism. Word and deed are *equally necessary, mutually interdependent and inseparable ministries, each carried out with the single purpose of the spread of the kingdom of God.'* [6] (italics mine)

Keller evades the question of precedent—'evangelism or mercy ministries?'—by using an illustration of 'repentance and baptism'. He writes: 'Which is more important—word or deed? Let's propose the possibility that differences arise on this issue because the very question of "importance" is misguided. For example, which commandment is more important: "repent" or "be baptised"? From one perspective we could say that the consequences of disobedience to the first command would be more disastrous than to the second. But would we be comfortable determining which of God's commands were more important to obey? Doesn't the very question create an unbiblical distinction within God's Word? So, too, it is an inappropriate to ask whether evangelism or social concern is more important. They constitute a whole that should not be divided.' [7] However, if we take baptism as a visible sign of *faith*, Keller could have spoken of 'repentance and faith' in the same way. If this is what he means then the parallel is only apparent and not real. Repentance and faith (of which baptism is a sacramental symbol) are two aspects of the same event——the appropriation of God's offer of salvation. The two are internally related to each other in that one is linked to the other in such a way that one does not become a possibility without the other. If repentance is a 'turning from' and faith a 'turning to', repentance is a necessary condition for faith, for in order to turn to face one direction logically necessitates a turning from the previous direction. On the other hand, if faith is also a perceiving that something is true (*assentus*), then faith logically precedes repentance as a necessary condition, a turning *from* that which is false, for unless one sees the truth one will not be aware that one has been following a lie.

But evangelism and social concern are *not* related in this way. They are two distinct activities not two aspects of the same event. In which case it *is* legitimate to ask, which is more important? Clearly the Bible itself does distinguish between things of first importance and secondary importance, even if they are both divine commands. In Hosea 6:6 we read: 'I desire mercy and not sacrifice.' This would indicate that in terms of priority it is mercy that God is looking for rather than ritual sacrifice, although he did command the latter. It could be argued that the ideal is both (cf. Luke 11:42), but that does not detract from the point that priorities do exist and that to ask such question is not, in the words of Dr Keller, to 'create an unbiblical distinction in God's Word.'

The questions are whether evangelism has priority over social action or vice versa or whether the two are of equal importance? Keller speaks of them being '*equally necessary* ministries' which still allows for one being more important than the other. [8]

This raises the question: by what criteria does one determine primacy even in a situation of double necessity?

Keller refers to three cases where, he claims, it is argued that evangelism has primacy over mercy: First, where mercy is a means to the end of evangelism; second, where mercy is only to be done in some circumstances; and thirdly, the biblically ordained time sequence of word and deed. All three, he maintains, cannot be substantiated biblically. But the most obvious argument for the primacy of evangelism is not considered, which is in terms of what is ultimately at stake, namely, people's eternal destiny. When this is placed into the equation, evangelism's primacy becomes self-evident. The test which can be applied is a simple theoretical one: given no alternative but a straightforward choice between sharing the Gospel with someone who is dying and alleviating their physical condition which should we do? The answer must be to share the Gospel if we take eternal realities seriously. Mark 1:38 is still a crucial text which has to be reckoned with. In response to Peter's implied demand that Jesus should heal the sick which were queuing up in Capernaum he replied, 'Let us go somewhere else-to the nearby villages-so that I might preach there also.' What is more, unless one is going to take signs and wonders as being evidence of mercy ministries (which Keller seems to do), the apostle Paul did not follow this pattern—in Athens or Thessalonica or indeed, in Corinth. Of course, depending upon the circumstances this did not prevent Paul from engaging in acts of mercy—e.g. Acts 28:7 with the inhabitants of Malta. But this hardly constitutes evidence that Paul views Gospel proclamation and mercy ministries as being equally necessary like the two wings of a plane, to use Keller's illustration. [9] In I Corinthians 9:16 Paul exclaims, 'Woe to me if I do not preach the gospel!' Paul never says, 'Woe to me if I do not engage in acts of mercy'. Certainly if faced with a need which he did not respond to then he would be guilty of lack of love, as well as cutting the throat of his Gospel proclamation by undermining his integrity. In this Keller is quite right, 'You tend to your friend because you love him' and not as a means to some other end. But given that Paul shared his life with the Thessalonians and treated them like a nurse with her children (1 Thessalonians 2:7), this indicates this was not the case. This simply means that in terms of integrity, deeds go with words. Keller carries his readers along by assuming that 'deeds' equals 'mercy ministries' which they do not.

How we are to conceive evangelism as being primary along with social action being necessary is well put by Michael Hill, 'While social action is necessary there is a sense in which evangelism is primary. God's rule and kingdom is not brought about by social action. People enter the kingdom and come under God's rule by hearing and responding to the Gospel. Evangelism is primary in a temporal sense. One has to be brought under the explicit rule of God and transformed by the gospel before one becomes a member of the people of God. But once people are brought into the community of believers where God rules they are transformed by the Spirit and the fruits of the Spirit will manifest themselves. The logic of God's domain requires its members to be committed to the good of all people. The relationship of evangelism to social action is analogous to the relationship between the entry point to a structure and the environment within the structure. Entry to God's domain is logically tied up with the shape of God's domain. A commitment to love and social action follows from coming under God's rule.'[10] However, Hill goes on to sound a note of caution; 'Even conceding that evangelism is primary in a very limited sense has its dangers. Such thinking might deny the logical link between evangelism and social action. It might suggest that there could be a choice between the two. Furthermore, it could recommend that evangelism is the only legitimate preference. To suggest this option would be like suggesting that one can enter the house and not be subject to the boundaries of the house. The reality is that evangelism will lead to conversion and conversion will lead to a new creation and that new creation will oblige people to be involved in social action.'[11] This logical link is illustrated by the parable of the Good Samaritan, but not quite in the way Keller proposes. A less ambitious understanding can still secure the same demands in practice for ministries of mercy.

Rhetoric and the Parable of the Good Samaritan

It is tempting to go straight to the parable for a lesson in ethics. But the context in which the parable is told is crucial for its theological understanding which is the issue of *salvation*. This is apparent in the lawyer's question as well as the parable itself which has some key Christological implications.

The occasion is the deceitful testing of Jesus by an expert in the law—v. 25: 'And behold, a lawyer stood up to put him to the test, saying, "Teacher, what shall I do to inherit eternal life?"' The normal teaching position of a rabbi was to sit and the pupil to stand as a sign of respect and recite the teaching. Here the position of standing is feigned for the true motive we are told was to examine the teacher. The natural question for the Rabbi would have been, 'How can I obey God?' But here the question is 'What must I do to inherit eternal life?' Presumably the questioner hoped that Jesus would say something injudicious against the Law of Moses. The fact that Jesus refuses to give a straight answer, but adopts a more Socratic method to elicit an answer from the lawyer himself, suggests that Jesus was wise to what the lawyer was attempting to do. However, the original question as it stands is misplaced. One *does* nothing to inherit, an inheritance is simply received. By its very nature it is a gift. So, therefore, is eternal life.

However, in response the lawyer does relate back to Jesus his summary of the law in verse 27 (cf. Matthew 7:12), to which Jesus replies, 'Do this and you will live.' Here Jesus raises the bar to an impossible level—unqualified love of God and neighbour, and so again underscoring the need for grace for anyone to qualify for the inheritance. This is not appreciated by the lawyer who seeks some definitions in order to fulfil the law, specifically 'Who is my neighbour?' For, we are told, the lawyer sought to 'justify himself.' Justification means to be saved, to inherit eternal life. He seeks a meritorial basis for his salvation. The lawyer would have his own views of what constitutes a neighbour based upon Leviticus 19:18, from which the summary is taken, 'You shall not take vengeance or bear a grudge against the sons of your own people, but you shall love your neighbour as yourself: I am the LORD.' Or in the wider context this could be extended beyond 'the sons of your own people' given verse 34, 'You shall treat the stranger who sojourns with you as the native among you, and you shall love him as yourself, for you were strangers in the land of Egypt: I am the LORD your God' Either way the neighbour could be carefully construed as being limited in scope. Jesus response is to tell the classic parable by using what K. E. Bailey calls 'the prophetic rhetorical template' [12] with seven scenes in all (the perfect number) with the climax being denoted at the centre with the last three scenes paralleling and inverting the first three scenes. This is shown below: [13]

1. A man was going down from Jerusalem to Jericho,
   And he fell among robbers.   ROBBERS
   And they stripped him and beat him   Steal and injure
   And departed, leaving him half dead.

   2. By coincidence a certain priest
      Was going down that road,   PRIEST
      And when he saw him,   See
      He passed by on the other side.   Do nothing

      3. Likewise also a certain Levite came to that place   LEVITE
         And when he saw him,   See
         He passed by on the other side.   Do nothing

         4. A certain Samaritan, travelling, came to him,   SAMARITAN
            And when he saw him he had compassion   See
               on him   Shows compassion

      5. He went to him,
         And bound up his wounds,   TREAT WOUNDS
         Pouring on oil and wine.   (The Levite's failure)

   6. Then he put him on his own animal   TRANSPORTING THE
      And led him to the inn,   MAN
      And took care of him.   (The Priest's failure)

7. The next day he took out and gave two denarii to the   SPEND MONEY ON HIM
   Manager and said, 'Take care of him, and whatever more   (Compensating for
   you spend I, on my return, will repay you.'   the thieves)

'Which of the three do you think proved a neighbour to the man who fell among the robbers?' He said, 'The one who showed mercy on him.' And Jesus said to him, 'Go and do likewise.'

The parallels are evident and the structure of the story is classically chiastic with the climax in the centre which is the compassion of the Samaritan. Bailey skilfully presents the cultural background to the parable.

There are certain expectations regarding the travellers. The Jerusalem temple was served by three groups: the Priest, who would have travelled by horse (thus being able to provide transport for the wounded man); the Levite, who would have had oil and wine in his pack normally used for cultic purposes; and the Jewish layman. So after the appearance and failure of the first two, the next person the hearers would have expected to appear was a Jewish layman. This is similar to the expectations involved in someone telling a joke concerning four men, an Englishman, Irishman, Welshman—and the fourth person would be expected to be a Scotsman. The shock comes in fact that it is not a Jewish layman at all but a hated Samaritan! (The wounded man in the story is assumed to be a Jewish layman coming down from Jerusalem and therefore certainly comes under the Leviticus 19 rubric). Mitigating circumstances might have been pleaded for the lack of responsiveness by the Priest and the Levite, not least in becoming ceremonially defiled by touching what may have been a dead body, a risk, they thought, not worth taking. The Levite would have been aware that the Priest would have passed this way before him and not taken action. The Levite could hardly consider himself to be more conversant with the requirements of the law than the Priest and so decided not to upstage him, for that would have be an act of insult to the priest. The safest course of action is to pass by.

The saving agent in the story is an outsider—a Samaritan. The primary motivating force for the Samaritan was not obedience to the law but compassion towards a person in need (and in so doing he obeyed the law). What he did was costly and involved risk. It was costly in that he used all the available resources he had to meet the man's needs (oil, wine, cloth wrapping, riding animal, energy and money). It was risky on two counts. First, by stopping to help he exposed himself to the risk of being attacked himself. There was no reason to suppose that bandits were not still in the area. Secondly, he risked his life transporting the man to an inn

within Jewish territory. This would have been equivalent to a black
man walking into a whites only hotel in the Southern States of
America at the height of segregation when the Ku Klux Clan
were still active and at large. He may have been expected to take
the man in the direction of Jericho and unload him on the edge
of the town. But to walk into the town and then further into an
inn was an unthinkable and dangerous thing to do. What is more,
the Samaritan ensured that the wounded man was not placed at
risk by taking on a further risk himself—v. 35, for he covered all
his needs and agreed to *return* to a hostile situation to cover any
further expenses. The risk that the wounded man was potentially
open to was being sold into slavery by the inn keeper if he were not
able to pay his bills.[14] The Samaritan spared him from this danger.
To say that the Samaritan displayed costly love would be a major
understatement.

Thus Jesus does not answer the Lawyer's question, 'Who is my
neighbour?' But indicates what it means to be a neighbour (costly
sacrifice) and to whom we become a neighbour (those in need with
whom we have to do).

It is not allegorising the parable to see within it echoes of Jesus'
own person and mission, as we similarly see in the parables of
Luke 15.[15] Israel's religious leaders fail in the story and salvation is
brought by someone breaking in from outside. What is more, the
'salvation' is costly and complete. Both aspects are fulfilled by Jesus
in the overall narrative of Luke. He is the one who is the perfect
neighbour coming in from the outside, not a member of the
religious establishment which, as represented by the lawyer, have
failed the 'people of the land', those who cannot help themselves.
The cost is the cross and the rescue is total and guaranteed—the
inheritance of eternal life.

Thus, while the Gospel is alluded to by the parable in the
context of Luke—the person and work of Christ—social action
can't be equated with the Gospel. What we have is an indication of
some of the Gospel entailments in the way suggested by Michael
Hill. Those who have been the recipients of the 'Good Samaritan'
par excellence, the Lord Jesus Christ, cannot deny that by ignoring
need in whatever form that might take—physical, spiritual, social

or mental.[16] But it is not simply a matter of 'walking the walk' and commending the Gospel by action (and avoid denying it by inaction) it is simply a matter of obedience. To walk on the other side is breaking God's command of loving one's neighbour as oneself. What is more, compassion is to be the motive using whatever resources are available to us, and in some cases, making resources available. To quote Hill, '…social action is not an option. The believer has been transformed into the image of Christ. Love is the essence of this new nature. Hence the Christian is commanded to do good to all people. And since all people's good is tied up with the cluster of relationships they share and the structures (patterns of relationship) shaping those relationships, Christians must be involved in social action, not only to express their new nature in Christ but to witness to the values of the Kingdom.'[17]

Given that the church is the gathering of Christians which as a community will organise activities and structures in order to serve God and the world, then it is right that churches consider how they are to meet the needs of their neighbours. Keller's book is well placed to be a valuable aid to church leaders to make the practical steps necessary for this to happen.[18] No doubt many ministries of mercy will be carried out on an individual level by members of a congregation. But this should not make the church leadership complacent in leaving matters there. The evangelical churches which emphasise evangelism in line with its Biblical priority would not be content to leave witness to the ad hoc day-to-day witness of its members but tend to invest vast amounts of time, money, energy and personnel in organised corporate evangelism, so why should social action be treated any differently?

At this point the question of resources is raised. Given that a church has only so many people, and so much time and money, to divert resources from evangelism to social action might be considered untenable. In some cases this might be so, although it does not rule out making some modest attempt at meeting social need—to use the language of the parable, we may only have oil to clean a wound and not wine, but we can use what we have. However, what is often the barrier is not lack of resources but motivation (the same can and often does apply to evangelism—

it is not that a small church can't do *any* evangelism because of
lack of resources, it opts to do *no* evangelism because of lack of
motivation). This, one would suspect, is where the problem lies for
those evangelical churches which do have plenty of resources but
choose to place them almost entirely at the disposal of evangelism
and edification. Maybe what is required here is a sacrificing of
some things (do we really need a full-time music leader?) in order
to supply something which may be less 'in vogue' in evangelical
circles but clearly in line with what the parable Jesus told demands
(e.g. a full-time social action worker)? Perhaps an excessive
amount is spent on evangelism in terms of publicity, venues and
arrangements which, to be frank, could be avoided and the money
allocated elsewhere.[19]

The fact that a church will have to reallocate its resources is no
excuse for inactivity on the social action front. To fail to respond
to this demand would be akin to the Priest ensuring that he is
not inconvenienced from carrying out his cultic duties by having
to deal with the dying man. The pressure to play the Priest in
keeping the 'evangelical show on the road' is a strong one—that
is, a 'show' characterised by acceptable activities—bible teaching,
fellowship groups and prayer for example (important though they
are). Furthermore, the pressure to play the Levite is also equally
strong ('who am I to dare to question the wisdom of those better
schooled than I?') so that matters of social concern are not raised
in the church for fear of being thought to be 'going off'.

Reducing the moral distance

In considering priorities in the church's ministry, strategy and
allocation of resources, the matter of 'moral distance' is raised.
Following through the parable of the Good Samaritan we spoke
of the obligation to meet the needs of those 'with whom we have
to do'. Is this simply those we come into immediate contact with
or is it a much wider circle?

The ethicist Peter Singer questions whether the notion of
moral distance is relevant to our global village. He writes: 'To
challenge my students to think about the ethics of what we owe
to people in need, I ask them to imagine that their route to the

university takes them past a shallow pond. One morning, I say to them, you notice a child has fallen in and appears to be drowning. To wade in and pull the child out would be easy but it will mean that you get your clothes wet and muddy, and by the time you go home and change you will have missed your first class. I then ask the students: do you have any obligation to rescue the child? Unanimously, the students say they do. The importance of saving a child so far outweighs the cost of getting one's clothes muddy and missing a class, that they refuse to consider it any kind of excuse for not saving the child. Does it make a difference, I ask, that there are other people walking past the pond who would equally be able to rescue the child but are not doing so? No, the students reply, the fact that others are not doing what they ought to do is no reason why I should not do what I ought to do. Once we are all clear about our obligations to rescue the drowning child in front of us, I ask: would it make any difference if the child were far away, in another country perhaps, but similarly in danger of death, and equally within your means to save, at no great cost— and absolutely no danger—to yourself? Virtually all agree that distance and nationality make no moral difference to the situation. I then point out that we are all in that situation of the person passing the shallow pond: we can all save lives of people, both children and adults, who would otherwise die, and we can do so at a very small cost to us: the cost of a new CD, a shirt or a night out at a restaurant or concert, can mean the difference between life and death to more than one person somewhere in the world—and overseas aid agencies like Oxfam overcome the problem of acting at a distance.'[20]

Singer makes a powerful point. It is not that Singer is denying that there is such a thing as 'moral distance'—one would be obligated to meet the need of someone who lies on your 'Jericho Road' but *not* someone who lies beyond your reach—rather, the argument is that our present situation is such that such 'distances' can be reduced to vanishing point. Therefore, for instance a church may decide that the immediate social need in its area which it can attempt to meet is the alleviation of debt through counselling. Accordingly, resources are channelled into this worthy cause. The geographical distance is small and so is the moral distance—i.e. the obligation to offer assistance even to a stranger. But the church may also decide to assist in the relief of street children in Bogota through financing some intermediate agency. Here the geographical distance is great but the moral distance, by an act of volition, has been reduced. The decision has been made to assist on a 'Jericho Road' on the other side of the world.

Summary

The parable of the Good Samaritan at one level reflects the nature of Christ's saving mission to the world; it comes from the outsider, costly, full and free. It also stands as a paradigm for the Christian and churches to 'go and do likewise'. There is being the good neighbour in sharing the Gospel at whatever cost with whomever we can. The need for salvation is real and the message of the cross-work of Christ alone meets that need. But there are other needs also. Here there is the challenge for evangelical churches in particular to reassess their ministry in this regard. Risk is integral to such an enterprise as is cost, but neither will be considered without the deeper wellspring of compassion. Perhaps it is lack of vitality in this affection which places some evangelical ministry in the position of the man who lies beaten on the road rather than the one who is able to offer assistance.

Endnotes

1. Tim Keller, *Ministries of Mercy* (Phillipsburg, NJ: P&R publishing, 1989) Second edition. Since the publication of this volume, Dr Keller has amplified further what he considers to be the church's dual mission of preaching the Gospel and promoting justice, in *Generous Justice: How God's Grace Makes us Just* (London: Hodder and Stoughton, 2010) and *Centre Church: Doing Balanced Gospel Centred Ministry in Your City* (Grand Rapids, Michigan: Zondervan, 2012).

2. We shall draw on the insightful work of Kenneth E. Bailey in his *Jesus through Middle Eastern Eyes—Cultural Studies in the Gospels'* (Leicester: IVP, 2008).

3. Op cit. p. 15

4. 'If among you, one of your brothers should become poor, in any of your towns within your land that the LORD your God is giving you,

you shall not harden your heart or shut your hand against your poor brother ... For there will never cease to be poor in the land. Therefore I command you, "You shall open wide your hand to your brother, to the needy and to the poor, in your land".'

5. Op cit. p. 13

6. Op cit. p. 106

7. Op cit. p. 109

8. Op cit. p. 109

9. Op cit. p. 110

10. Michael Hill, 'An Evangelical Rationale for Social Action', produced by the Social Issues Committee for the Anglican Diocese of Sydney, http://www.sie.org.au/pdf/reports/Hill_M_Evangelical_Rationale_1998.pdf, p. 13

11. Ibid. p. 13

12. Bailey, op cit, p. 290

13. Ibid. p. 291

14. Ibid. p. 292

15. Kenneth Bailey, *Prodigal and the Cross*, (Leicester: IVP, 2005).

16. Similarly, Tim Keller can write: 'Jesus is the Great Samaritan to whom the Good Samaritan points', *Generous Justice*, p. 77

17. Hill, op cit. p. 12

18. See also *Generous Justice*, pp. 112-147

19. Whilst offering some helpful criticisms of Dr Keller's view of the mission of the church, it would seem that Peter J. Naylor unhelpfully overstates his case somewhat when he writes, 'Even modest social tasks can soak up the energies of a congregation. But it will also find its concentration on preaching the gospel and personal witnessing becomes diluted', Peter J. Naylor, 'The Church's Mission' in *Engaging with Keller* eds. Iain D. Campbell and William M. Schweitzer, (Darlington, Evangelical Press, 2013). This is not necessarily so as Keller's own church demonstrates very clearly.

20. Peter Singer, 'The Drowning Child and the Expanding Circle'. *The New Internationalist*, Issue 289.

5

Theological Reflections

A way forward

It may be of value to reflect theologically on some of the proposals made in recent years regarding the relation between evangelism and social action as well as indicating a way forward for a more biblically grounded understanding.

Evangelism and Social action— two wings/two blades?

We have already seen how Dr Tim Keller likens evangelism and social action to 'two wings of a plane' and indicated the inadequacy of this comparison. But this is only a slightly different illustration to that used by Dr John Stott in elaborating the Grand Rapids document when he speaks of evangelism and social activity as a partnership, like 'two blades of a pair of scissors' or 'two wings of a bird', while earlier on insisting that evangelism had a logical and theological priority.[1]

On reflection this position appears untenable.

The very imagery used negates the claim that evangelism has priority. Can one say which blade of a pair of scissors is more important? Not at all, both are of equal importance for without both blades the pair of scissors would simply cease to *be* scissors, let alone function. Similarly, can one speak of one bird's wing having priority? Again the answer is no, since both are equally necessary

for the bird to fly at all. Perhaps unthinkingly, social action has
been exalted to the same status as evangelism, and, as we have
seen, neither Wesley nor Wilberforce would countenance such a
notion. But this is an inconsistency for elsewhere in the Grand
Rapids report it is stated explicitly that: 'Evangelism relates to
people's eternal destiny [no mention here of social activity], and
in bringing them the good news of salvation, Christians are doing
what nobody else can do. Seldom if ever should we have to choose
between healing bodies and saving souls ... Nevertheless, if we
must choose, then we have to say that the supreme and ultimate
need of all humankind is the saving grace of Jesus Christ'

But such a claim is undermined by talk of evangelism and social
action being 'in reality a marriage'.

Dr John Woodhouse's comment on this point is particularly
apposite:

> The significant disagreement among evangelicals has to do with the
> motivation that has been advanced for our social concern. On the
> one side of the debate, a perceived neglect of social responsibilities
> is redressed by arguing that social action is more significant than
> evangelicals have hitherto acknowledged. It is a worthwhile
> question to ask whether in the proposed heyday of evangelical social
> action—last century—the kind of theological justification advanced
> today was present. My impression is that it was not on the other side
> of the debate, it is acknowledged that to love one's neighbour is a
> Christian duty ... And who would deny that we have neglected our
> duties. It is right that we should be called again and again to care.
> But when that obligation is given the theological undergirding that
> belongs properly to the task of evangelism, when the evangelistic
> task is no longer seen as unique in importance, when evangelistic
> responsibility is taken for granted, and our neglect of social causes
> deeper remorse than our neglect of evangelism, then the cart has
> been put before the horse and is trying to grow legs.[2]

A cautionary tale is told by Professor Don Carson of an
assessment made by a Mennonite leader of his own movement,
namely, that one generation of Mennonites cherished the gospel
and *believed* that the *entailment* of the gospel lay in certain social
and political commitments. The next generation *assumed* the

gospel and *emphasized* the social and political commitments. The present generation *identifies* itself with the social and political commitments, while the gospel is variously confessed or disowned, it no longer lies at the heart of the belief system of some who call themselves Mennonites. Carson comments: 'Whether or not this is a fair reading of the Mennonites, it is certainly a salutary warning for evangelicals at large.'[3]

Tim Chester's assessment of the inadequacies of the 'two wings' approach of Stott and, by extension the 'two wings' illustration by Keller, is pertinent and to the point, 'Many evangelicals want to argue that evangelism and social action are equal activities. They describe evangelism and social action as two wings of a bird or the blades of a pair of scissors. While evangelism and social action are partners in many situations, it is inadequate to think of them as corresponding activities of equal impact ... the greatest need of the poor, as it is for all people, is to be reconciled with God and escape his wrath. Only the message of the gospel can do this. The adage, often attributed to St Francis of Assisi, 'Preach the gospel, use words if necessary' will not do. Social action can demonstrate the gospel, but without the communication of the gospel message, social action is like a signpost pointing nowhere. Indeed without the message of the gospel it points in the wrong direction. If we only do good works among people, then we point to ourselves and our charitable acts. People will think well of us but not of Jesus Christ. We may even convey the message that salvation is achieved by good works. Or we may convey the message that what matters most is economic and social betterment. We must not do social action without evangelism.'[4]

A similar endorsement of the relationship between evangelism and social action whilst esteeming evangelism's priority is found in Michael Hill's, *An Evangelical Rationale for Social Action:*

> Social action is a necessary part of the Christian life. Becoming a new creature in Christ transforms a person, making them other-person centred and loving. Social action flows from love and is an aspect of doing good to others. Since people are social and relational beings their good is found not only in right personal relationships but in the social structures which frame those relationships. While

social action is necessary there is a sense in which evangelism is primary. God's rule and kingdom is not brought about by social action. People enter the kingdom and come under God's rule by hearing and responding to the gospel. Evangelism is primary in a temporal sense. One has to be brought under the explicit rule of God and transformed by the gospel before one becomes a member of the people of God. But once people are brought into the community of believers where God rules they are transformed by the Spirit and the fruits of the Spirit will manifest themselves. The logic of God's domain requires its members to be committed to the good of all people. The relationship of evangelism to social action is analogous to the relationship between the entry point to a structure and the environment within the structure. Entry to God's domain is logically tied up with the shape of God's domain. A commitment to love and social action follows from coming under God's rule. There is no point to entering a right relationship if one is not going to be subject to the demands of that relationship. Evangelism cannot be an end in itself. Evangelism, when it meets a positive response, leads to a right relationship with God and that relationship has to be lived out otherwise there is no point to entering it. Evangelism and social action are like shape and size, you can't have one without the other. [5]

Hill has the balance about right.

Creation-Redemption and Eschatology

In some quarters there is a tendency to separate creation from redemption such that our obligations for social action only arise out of our obligations to God as Creator. On the other hand, some collapse the doctrines of creation and redemption into each other with the resulting view that the Kingdom of God itself is advanced through the renewing of the structures of society. At different stages in his career, John Gladwin, the former Bishop of Guildford, has argued for both positions.

In 1979, he wrote, 'It is because this is God's world and he cared for it to the point of incarnation and crucifixion that we are inevitably committed to work for God's justice in the face of oppression, for God's truth in the face of lies and deceits, for service in the face of the abuse of power, for love in the face of selfishness, for co-operation in the face of destructive antagonism, and for reconciliation in the face of division and hostility. The motivating power is the love of Christ which has gripped our hearts and consciences. This love is what drives people to get immersed in the messy business of politics and social shaping.'[6]

John Woodhouse simply raises the question, 'Why is it, then, that we do not find the Bible arguing like this?'[7] Woodhouse goes on to point out that it is by virtue of God being our Creator that he is our Judge, and so this is one good enough reason to be concerned with sharing the Gospel. Also, as a fellow creature, we are obliged to care for other people's needs, including the great spiritual need of salvation. The Bible does not split 'creation' and 'redemption' so as to yield different obligations.

Later in his career in an article entitled, *Towards a New Social Revolution*, Gladwin sees the doctrine of the Kingdom of God as being decisive in not only offering motivation for social involvement but indicating what shape it might take, 'Kingdom thinking is about more than simply following the example of Jesus in His acts of mercy for the needy … it is concerned with the structures of society, their inability to reform themselves and the need, therefore, for confrontation with them and for radical change of them … Kingdom patterns remind the church that it is not only concerned with *preserving* the social order, not even only with providing it with an *alternative*, but also that it is concerned with the radical transformation of social order.'[8]

Again we may simply ask, why doesn't the Bible argue this way? As we have seen, the Kingdom of God is that sphere in which there is salvation and as such is more or less synonymous with the Lordship of Christ which is advanced by the proclamation of the Gospel. The concern for 'the *radical* transformation of the social order' is not within its purview, except in terms of its consummation.

Is it not possible to recapture the simple spirit and evangelical convictions of the past which arise out of Scripture, so that we can be effective in the present in the light of things to come? After all, the one who said 'Go and make disciples of all nations' is the same Lord who said 'Fill the earth and subdue it', he is One Lord, Creator and Redeemer. [9]

The Insight of Biblical Theology

It has been suggested that a biblical theory of ethics shaped by biblical theology might provide a basis for such convictions. [10]

Michael Hill argues that the shape of biblical theology is always teleological, that is, moving towards a goal: 'The Bible story begins with an order in creation governed by the purpose of God. The story goes on to tell of the fracturing of that order and the neglect of the purposes of God. Wonderfully it tells of the one obedient man who upholds and fulfils the design of the Father. Knowledge of God's purposes is restored and the means of recovery established. Kinds and purposes find their true relationship in Jesus. The substance of morality is found in the value of kinds and the true nature of kinds is only detected in their goal or telos ... the goal of creation is the Kingdom of God. The nature of the kingdom is spelt out in terms of harmonious relationships.' [11]

Hill rightly maintains that strictly speaking Christian ethics is about applying biblical moral standards to those who have been made new creatures in Christ. But in the world where not all are committed to the Lordship of Christ, the goal of Christian ethics—a community of mutual love relationships—is not always achievable, so 'retrieval ethics' operates in situations less than ideal. The corollary of this would be that until the consummation of the Kingdom, society might well be reformed and brought closer into line with God's creative purposes, not least through Christian involvement as an expression of neighbourly love, but it cannot be said to have been *redeemed,* that is a term properly applied to the Christian community, a point which, as we noted, was made by Sir Norman Anderson at NEAC 1.

When we turn to Paul's letter to the Colossians with its distinctive emphasis on the unitary activity of God as Creator-Redeemer, we discover that many of the theological themes noted by Hill, and which shaped the thinking and action of the Reforming Evangelicals, are very much to the fore.

First, thanksgiving is offered to God the Father because of the Christians' faith and love which springs from their future hope which has broken into their lives through the message of the gospel (Colossians 1:3–8). This in turn leads on to intercession that fruit 'in every good work' be borne so that the believers may live lives worthy of the Lord, given their new status as members of the Kingdom of God's Son (1:9–13). This Son is not only redeemer but the one through whom all things were created, he is the heir of the universe, the one for whom it was made. Those once alienated from God have been reconciled by his atoning death with a view to being presented to God as holy, a destiny guaranteed if they hold on to the gospel of hope (1:15–23). The commission given to Paul to present the Word of God in its fullness, which means presenting Christ, entails suffering. Christians are to resist being lured away by hollow philosophies, but to persist in Christ (1:24–2:23). In keeping with their new status in Christ, these believers are to be heavenly minded, which involves putting to death desires and practices which arise out of our fallen nature and to put on attitudes and practices which accord with their new nature (3:1–14). These are to work themselves out not only within the community of the redeemed, but also the wider spheres of social relationships in the home and work (3:15–4:1). What is more, there is to be an outflow into what we would call evangelism, so that Paul can ask that prayers be made on the apostles' behalf that God will open a door of opportunity for gospel proclamation and that the Colossian believers themselves might know how they might act towards outsiders, making the best of every opportunity with a view to sharing their faith verbally (4:1–6).

In other words, it is the priority of the gospel of redemption which, when rightly appropriated, leads to both evangelism *and* social action as naturally as a seed when planted produces both leaves and flowers (Colossians 1:6). But given that evangelism is the planting of the gospel seed which gives rise to further evangelism and what might be broadly termed social action, there is a certain logical necessity, not to say theological necessity, for evangelism to be given pride of place within the life and purposes of the church.

The theological co-ordination of evangelism and social ethics—an insight by Karl Barth

Is there a better way of understanding the relationship between evangelism and social action than that proposed either by the heirs of Lausanne or the Radical evangelicals which accords more closely to the general tenor of Scripture? I would suggest that there is and it is one based on a concept proposed by Karl Barth. [12]

Barth argues that God's activity in the world has a centre and circumference. The centre is the coming of God's kingdom in Jesus Christ, the circumference around this centre is God's gracious providential rule of all things.

When it is asked what activity of man corresponds to God's overruling providence at the circumference. The answer is work. God in his Fatherly providence sustains, directs and cares for his world. Therefore, our work is about sustaining, directing and caring for the world.

Just as God's providence surrounds and supports the centre of his action in the coming Kingdom in Jesus Christ, so our human work should surround and support our service of the Kingdom. Sometimes, of course, the two coincide, as in the case of a full-time Christian minister which would run parallel to the ministry of Christ whose work was service. Also, a point will come when the Kingdom of God and creation are at one, with the establishment of the new creation towards which salvation history is moving.

This model is extremely helpful in enabling us to grasp the relation between evangelism and social action. Intuitively, Stott recognizes this relation, but in order to give social involvement a greater prominence in evangelical thinking than perhaps it has had at some points in its recent history, that which lies at the circumference had been drawn into the centre and the result was an unstable tension. The Radical Evangelicals, on the other hand, *extend* the centre out to the circumference so that *all* of God's activity is viewed as Kingdom activity. But the advantage of Barth's model is that while recognizing that creation and redemption belong together, as does God's providential activity and his specific saving activity, [13] they are nonetheless to be distinguished, such that God's providential work *serves* his saving work. Because evangelism is central to the extension of his Kingdom, in a way that, say, a Christian politician forming political policy is not, evangelism has priority over social involvement in that it belongs to the centre of God's activity in the world. This seems to accord well with the New Testament representation, to which we now turn beginning with Jesus' own teaching in the Sermon on the Mount.

ENDNOTES

1. John R. W. Stott, *The Contemporary Christian* (Leicester: IVP, 1992), pp 339-40

2. John Woodhouse 'Evangelism and Social Responsibility' B. G. Webb (ed.) *Christians in Society* Exploration 3 (Lancer 1998) pp 19-20

3. D. A. Carson, *The Cross in Christian Ministry* (Grand Rapids, Michigan: Baker, 1993) p. 63

4. Tim Chester, *Good New to the Poor: the Gospel through social Involvement* (Leicester: IVP, 2004)

5. Michael Hill, 'An Evangelical Rationale for Social Action', p. 13 http://www.sie.org.au/pdf/reports/Hill_M_Evangelical_Rationale_1998.pdf

6. *John Gladwin, 'God's People in God's World: Biblical Motives for Social Involvement'* (Leicester: IVP, 1979), p. 125

7. Op cit. p. 20

8. Cited in Rachel Tingle 'Evangelical Social Action Today: Road to Recovery or Road to Ruin?' *The Anglican Evangelical Crises,* Melvin Tinker (ed.) (Fearn, Ross-shire: Christian Focus Publications, 1995)

9. For a discussion on how Christian ethics might be commended to society at large see, M. Tinker 'The Priority of Jesus' teaching and example in Christian Ethics' *Themelios* Vol 13 No 1 1987

10. Michael Hill, 'Biblical Theology and Ethics in Interpreting God's Plan'— *Biblical Theology and the Pastor,* R. J. Gibson (ed) (Paternoster Press 1998) pp. 91-109

11. Ibid. p. 107-108

12. Karl Barth, *Church Dogmatics III 4* (Edinburgh: T and T Clark, 1978) pp. 565 ff

13. See, Paul Helm, *The Providence of God* (Leicester: IVP, 1993), Chapter 4.

6

The Sermon on the Mount and the Lord's Servant

A way in to understanding the relationship between Evangelism and Social Action

Introduction

The Sermon on the Mount has occupied a pivotal place in the life of Christians since it was first preached on that remote Galilean hillside some 2,000 years ago. John Stott comments that it 'has a unique fascination. It seems to present the quintessence of the teaching of Jesus. It makes goodness attractive. It shames our shabby performance. It engenders dreams of a better world.'[1]

Similarly D. A. Carson writes, 'The more I read these chapters—Matthew 5, 6 and 7—the more I am both drawn to them and shamed by them. Their brilliant light draws me like a moth to the spotlight; but the light is so bright it sears and burns. No room is left for forms of piety which are nothing more than veneer and sham. Perfection is demanded. Jesus says, "Be perfect ... as your heavenly Father is perfect" (5:48).'[2]

The Sermon is sometimes referred to as the 'kingdom manifesto'. It is reasonable to assume that if we are to look for Jesus' own understanding of the stance his followers are to take in relation to the world, what their priorities and practices are meant to be, then, this would be a good place to start.

The Sermon on the Mount and
its Isaianic background

Jesus teaching in the section on the Sermon on the Mount
running from 5:13–16 in which he likens his disciples to salt
and light, has frequently been drawn upon not only to provide
a theological rationale for Christian social action but as being
suggestive of the means. Thus, John Stott can write: 'Both images
set the two communities (Christian and non-Christian) apart. The
world is dark, Jesus implied, but you are to be its light. The world is
decaying, but you are to be salt, and hinder its decay ... Although
Christians are (or should be) morally and spiritually distinct from
non-Christians, they are not to be socially segregated. On the
contrary, their light is to shine into darkness, and their salt to soak
into the decaying meat ... Before the days of refrigeration, salt
was the best known preservative ... Light is even more obviously
effective; when the light is switched on, the darkness is actually
dispelled. Just so, Jesus seems to have meant, Christians can hinder
social decay and dispel the darkness of evil.' [3] Without wishing
to deny that Christians can and do hinder social decay and dispel
evil in a society, it is doubtful that this is the way Jesus intended
these metaphors to function within the context of the address
given from the Mountain. What such interpretations as Stott's
tend to do is to understand 'salt' and 'light' as universal metaphors
and then read off their sense as presently understood (preservation
and illumination) and assume that this is what Jesus meant. This
carries the obvious danger of engaging in an anachronistic reading
of the text. What is more, the metaphors tend to be detached
from the wider canonical context and treated in isolation from
the more immediate literary context without exploring whether
there is any *theological* connection to be made between them. Also,
there is often a failure to note that Jesus in fact uses *three*, not
two pictures, for there is also a 'city on a hill.' What is necessary
is first to consider how this part of Jesus' discourse relates to the
immediate context; second to ask whether what is being said
has Old Testament associations and third, to tease out how such
metaphors function in relation to both considerations. This will
then enable us to more precisely identify the meaning of Jesus

teaching and its significance for his followers given that it is actual and prospective disciples which are in view. [4]

The wider picture

Let us first take matters of setting, background and context.

In Matthew's Gospel, the setting is the sermon delivered from the mountainside. Parallels between Jesus and Moses have often been made at this point [5] for example, the gathering of God's redeemed people before Mount Sinai, the delivering of God's Word to them by God's appointed mediator Moses, and so on. Without wishing to deny such allusions, I would suggest that they are secondary to the more striking points of contact which exist with the heralding Servant in Isaiah 40–66. The identification of Jesus as this Servant has already been made explicit at his baptism (Matthew 3:17). Jesus is then presented by Matthew as the great fulfilment figure with the quotation from Isaiah 9 in 4:14–16 who begins his ministry by proclaiming the Kingdom of heaven and the concomitant call to repent. This is in line with the mission of the Servant as found in the central sections of Isaiah who is given the task of announcing the arrival of God's reign in salvation (52:7), a salvation which is established through his teaching and suffering (50:4–11; 51:4, 16; 52:13–53:12 *passim*).

Matthew's relating of the ministry of Jesus which immediately precedes the Sermon on the Mount also testifies to the fulfilment of the Isaianic vision (Matthew 4:23–25). There we observe that there is an *outward* movement in which Jesus heralds the good news amongst people who had no difficulty at all in recognising their needy downtrodden state. At the same time as announcing the Kingdom he acted to lift people out of their needy situation as evidenced by healing the sick and liberating the demon possessed (4:24). There might also be a hint of the wider ministry of Jesus as a 'light to the Gentiles' by the passing reference that news spread all over *Syria*.

This is followed in the second place, by an *inward* movement: the gathering of Israel as represented by the large crowds of verse 25 which came from 'Galilee and the Decapolis, and from Jerusalem and Judea, and from beyond the Jordan.' (cf. Isaiah 60:4).

The commencement of Jesus' programmatic ministry in his hometown synagogue by Luke is well known with the assertion that the prophecy of Isaiah 61 had been fulfilled in the hearing of the congregation (Luke 4:16ff). What is not so readily recognised is that the *same* passage lies behind the beginning of Jesus public ministry in Matthew as represented by the Sermon on the Mount.

For example, a convincing case can be made that the first four beatitudes have their grounding in Isaiah 61:

'Blessed are the *poor* in spirit for theirs is the Kingdom of heaven.' (Matthew 5:3).

'The Spirit of the Lord God is upon me, because the Lord has anointed me to bring good news to the *poor*.' (Isaiah 61:1)

'Blessed are those who *mourn* for they shall be *comforted*.' (Matthew 5:4)

'He has sent me to bind up the broken-hearted, … to *comfort* all who *mourn*; to grant to those who mourn' (Isaiah 61:1–3).

'Blessed are the meek for they shall *inherit* the *earth*' (Matthew 5:5)

'Instead of your shame there shall be a double portion; instead of dishonour they shall rejoice in their lot (inheritance); therefore in their land they shall possess a double portion; they shall have everlasting joy (Isaiah 61:7)

'Blessed are those who hunger and thirst for *righteousness* for they shall be satisfied.' (Matthew 5:6)

'they may be called oaks of righteousness, the planting of the Lord' (Isaiah 61:3).[6]

There are other themes in Isaiah 61 and the surrounding chapters, 60 and 62, which have direct bearing on the three metaphors which Jesus goes on to use in v. 13ff which we shall return to in due course. At this point let it suffice to note that there are several themes and motifs which are common to both the Sermon on the Mount and the Servant Songs.[7]

It is, however, to his immediate circle of disciples as distinct from the larger crowd, that Jesus addresses his words.[8]

These are the ones described as 'blessed.' In the Greek translation of the Old Testament, known as the Septuagint (LXX), *'makarios'* renders the Hebrew comparative article, *'ashrey'*. It therefore functions as a *description* of a state of affairs rather than acting as a performative announcement which *brings into being* a state of affairs. As such, the addressees are the 'enviable ones' who are in a prized position. The fortunate situation in which they find themselves relates somehow to 'the 'Kingdom'—a term which constitutes the two 'book ends' of the beatitudes in verses 2 and 10 (technically called an *inclusio*). Given that the opening beatitude and the closing beatitude define the members of the Kingdom, it is to these we shall give some detailed attention.

Jesus describes as enviable those who are 'poor in the realm of the spirit.' This is not a description of people lacking spiritual things as such—having a spiritual deficiency of some kind—but a description of someone's lower standing in relation to someone else. *Ptochos* (poor) is a depressive word describing a person who is in a dependent-client relationship; it refers to the destitute who could only exist with the help of charitable assistance (e.g. Lazarus in Luke 16:20).[9] It is hardly likely that Jesus was applying this term to describe the physical poverty of his followers as by the standards of the day they were not poor at all, indeed, they carried a money bag and gave alms rather than received them.

The background is again Isaiah. Whilst most certainly the Messiah is presented as one who will be concerned with the physical poor whose state of poverty is a result of oppression and injustice, as we see for example in Isaiah 11:4; 61:8; 49:13, the term poor/afflicted ones (*ani*) has been extended to describe the *whole* nation which finds itself destitute and beggar-like in Exile as it stands in a dependent-client relationship with Yahweh, wholly dependent upon him for salvation. As Seccombe writes: 'Seeing Israel as poor became so intrinsic to national self-understanding that sectarian groups like the Qumran community could seize the title and actually name themselves "the Poor".'[10]

Thus the poor—*anihim* (LXX *ptochoi*) are those who are in a state of oppression and affliction; designated as being of lowly, humble status. This is the state which characterises the true people of God. [11] But why should this be described as a fortunate position to be in? The answer is that to such is promised the 'Kingdom'. With Isaiah 61 providing the theological backcloth to the beatitudes, what is being promised is the restoration of God's people—an end to Exile [12] and the announcement of the day of favour of Yahweh—the Jubilee. While this is a teaching open to all, it only becomes effective for those who identify themselves with Jesus. This will entail suffering which brings us to the final beatitude in verse 10 and its extended treatment in v. 11: 'Blessed are those who are persecuted because of righteousness for theirs is the Kingdom of heaven.'

We have already seen how the members of the Qumran community identified themselves as the poor. They described themselves as the '*ebyonim*', a term considered appropriate not as a moral quality but because of the 'affliction' they suffered which is the lot of the remnant of Israel. [13] The perfect tense is used to describe Jesus' followers as the persecuted ones, 'Blessed are those who *have been* persecuted' and so reinforcing the understanding this is something which will repeatedly occur. In verse 10 the persecution is said to arise because of righteousness, but in verse 11 it comes about on account of Jesus. In verse 12 a direct association is made with the former prophets, presumably because they were persecuted on account of righteousness also. This raises the question: what 'righteousness' did the prophets perform, and the disciples were about to perform, which leads to such opposition?

In the Old Testament, righteousness is that which is well pleasing to God and which receives approval in the heavenly court. [14] The connotation is not distributive justice, guaranteeing fairness so that each receives what is deserved, but rather acts on behalf of people who cannot help themselves. It is supremely in salvation, therefore, that God exhibits his righteousness (e.g. Isaiah 46:13: 'I bring near my righteousness; it is not far off, and my salvation will not delay; I will put salvation in Zion, for Israel my glory.'). As with John the Baptist who, 'Came ... in the way of righteousness' (Matthew

21:32) to 'turn many of the children of Israel to the Lord their God' (Luke 1:16) so is the 'saving righteousness' performed by all true prophets. It is this calling of people to covenant fidelity, a total way of life given over to the Creator-Redeemer God which fulfils the righteous saving purposes of God. [15]

It is noteworthy that the manner in which this persecution comes is 'insulting' and 'speaking evil.' The nature of the prophetic ministry is such that it is invariably met in this way. Why that should be so turns on what the nature of that ministry is, which, having just been touched on above, is elucidated further by the section which lies on the other side of Jesus' 'salt and light' sayings concerning 'the fulfilment of the law and the prophets'—Matthew 5:17–20.

In verse 17 Jesus says to his disciples, 'Do not think that I have come to abolish the law and/or the prophets; I have not come to abolish them but to fulfil them.' The use of the aorist subjunctive suggests that Jesus was heading off a future objection which might be raised in the light of his teaching rather than countering one currently being held by his followers. The identical term, 'law and the prophets' is used again in 7:12 forming an *inclusio* for the whole of this section and so strongly intimating that Jesus is emphasising continuity between former revelation and his present ministry, something which he goes on to expound at length. Also, from the fact that in verse 18 Jesus deals with the matter of the law alone, it would be legitimate to infer that the use of the term 'prophets' indicates that Jesus has in view the wider extension and application of the law, the 'spirit' as well as the 'letter', since it was the function of the prophets to correct the people's misapplication and neglect of their covenant obligations (as Jesus himself does in the remaining section running from 5:21–7:12). This aspect of the prophets' ministry is summarised in 2 Kings 17:13: 'The Lord warned Israel and Judah through all of his prophets and seers, 'Turn from your evil ways and keep my commandments and my statutes, in accordance with all the Law that I commanded your fathers, and that I sent to you by my servants the prophets.'

In what sense, therefore, do Jesus and his followers 'fulfil' the law and prophets? The word to fulfil (*pleroo*) occurs 16 times in

Matthew. Twelve of these occur in relation to the fulfilment of prophecy. The other three occasions—3:15; 13:48; 23:32 (not counting the one here in verse 17) indicate the completion and finality of something—the 'filling' of covenant obligations in baptism, the 'filling' of a net with fish, and the 'filling up' of God's judgement. And so it would seem that the meaning in verse 17 is that in the new age of the Messiah amongst the Messiah's new community the final expression of the law will be manifest—its telic end will be reached. [16] Theirs will be a righteousness which exceeds that of the Pharisees (v. 20), whose attitude was anticipated and condemned by Isaiah (Matthew 15:7) with their principle of 'minimum requirement' which is in the sights of much of Jesus' teaching in the following section. By way of contrast, Jesus in true prophetic style is concerned not only with outward action but inner attitude, motives as well as methods. He commends the principle of 'maximum application'. As the prophets in the past called God's people back to the true nature of their covenant obligations, not least in the realm of social justice, and were met with scorn and derision, so the followers of the Servant who exercise such a prophetic ministry will meet with the same.

To summarise: the Servant heralds good tidings from the mountain; it is the time when the Exile is ended and restoration begins for the people of God. The state of those who recognise their afflicted situation is one of great fortune for to them belongs the Kingdom. This paradoxical state of blessing/affliction will continue in the form of the persecution of those who carry out a prophetic/proclamatory ministry in the name of Christ. This happened with the former prophets and will continually re-occur as people are called to covenant fidelity. In this sense Jesus and his new community stand in direct line with the prophets of old and the righteousness spoken of in Isaiah 61 begins to be fulfilled amongst his followers.

ENDNOTES

1. J. R. W. Stott, *The Message of the Sermon on the Mount*, The Bible Speaks Today, (Leicester: IVP, 1978), p. 9

2. D. A. Carson, *The Sermon on the Mount. An Evangelical Exposition of Matthew 5-7* (Grand Rapids: Baker, 1978) p11.

3. John R. W. Stott, *Issues facing Christians Today* (Basingstoke: Marshall Pickering, 1984), p. 65

4. Note the withdrawing from the crowds and it is when his disciples came to him that we read:' And he opened his mouth and taught *them* saying …'

5. E.g. Vern S. Poythress, *The Shadow of Christ in the Law of Moses*, (New Jersey: P&R, 1991), Chapter 17.

6. W. J. Dumbrell has given some very helpful exegetical thoughts on the Old Testament background to the Sermon on the Mount in *'Seven Exegetical Studies in Matthew 5:1-17'* (Moore Theological College, Sydney).

7. 'There are many themes and motifs common to both the Sermon on the Mount and the Servant Songs: The Messiah as teacher, the declaration of the gospel from the mountain, the gathering of Israel, the salvation of the poor, the kingdom of God, satisfying the hungry, giving gladness and laughter to those who weep and mourn, the reproach of people, being cast out for the sake of the Servant's name, reward and consolation, the importance of hearing, the blind and those who see, turning the other cheek, the mercy of God, the coming of the light, obedience to the Servant.' David Seccombe, *The King of God's Kingdom. A solution to the puzzle of Jesus*, (Carlisle: Paternoster, 2002), p. 253.

8. Although, given the response of the crowds to his teaching in 7:28 caution should be exercised against making any hard and fast distinction between his immediate followers who are called to himself and the larger gathering of potential disciples.

9. See David Seccombe, *Possessions and the Poor in Luke-Acts*, (Linz: SNTU, 1983), p. 137

10. Seccombe, op.cit. p. 162.

11. This is a position argued in detail by Warren Heard Northbrook, II, 'Luke's Attitude Toward the Rich and the Poor' *A Puritan's Mind*, www.apuritansmind.com

12. The most notable advocate of this view is N. T. Wright in *Jesus and the Victory of God*, (London: SPCK, 1993). Also see, Mervyn Eloff, *From the Exile to the Christ*, Unpublished PhD Thesis, University of Stellenbosch) who argues that 'return from exile is a valid "hermeneutical prism" for the interpretation of Matthew's gospel' in its entirety.

13. 1 QM 14:7

14. See S. Motyer, 'Righteousness by faith in the New Testament' in, *Here We Stand* (J. I. Packer, ed.), (London: Hodder and Stoughton, 1986) p35.

15. Motyer writes of the Sermon on the Mount 'We are struck by the way Matthew does not distinguish between God's righteousness and man's. "Seek first his kingdom and his righteousness" probably does not refer primarily to the ethical righteousness which Jesus' disciples must seek to attain, but (in parallel with the 'kingdom') to the eschatological completion of God's salvation for which we yearn. If that is correct, then this will be the meaning of "Blessed are those who hunger and thirst after righteousness" (5:6) also. But it would be wrong to deny that in both these verses the thought is of righteousness resting upon man, for the longing expressed in 5:6 is to be caught up in God's saving purpose. Then 5:20 makes it clear that this places a rigorous ethical demand on us, "unless your righteousness exceeds that of the scribes and Pharisees, you will never enter the kingdom of heaven", and 6:1 NIV speaks simply of "your acts of righteousness". This ethical meaning fits in with Matthew's overall emphasis on the call to discipleship, and is always in mind when he uses the adjective *dikaios.*' Ibid. pp. 36-37.

16. See, Zoe Holloway, *'Understanding and Misunderstanding the Discontinuity that Christ Makes to the Moral Order and the Mosaic Law: A Conceptual Foundation for Using the Mosaic Law in Christian Ethics.'* Unpublished Thesis, Moore College Sydney.

7

More from Isaiah—Salt, Light and a City on a Hill

If we are going to truly understand what Jesus is saying in this sermon and how it is to work out amongst his followers then we need to delve a little deeper into its background from the prophet Isaiah and spend some time unpacking a little more carefully the pictures Jesus uses regarding his followers being like 'salt', 'light' and a 'city on a hill', especially since they are often appealed to by evangelicals as providing a basis for social involvement.

Isaiah and the Servant of the Lord

Isaiah 61 links back to chapter 60 and forward to chapter 62. Chapter 60:1–3 has the people gathering awaiting the return to Zion with the promise that, 'Nations shall come to your light, and kings to the brightness of your rising' Verses 4–11 picture the rebuilding of the city on a hill—Jerusalem. Towards the end in verses 21–22, we hear echoes of the Abrahamic covenant with references to the giving of the land and the growth of a mighty nation: 'Your people shall all be righteous; they shall possess the land forever, the branch of my planting, the work of my hands, that I might be glorified. The least one shall become a clan, and the smallest one a mighty nation; I am the Lord; in its time I will hasten it.' In chapter 62 the blessings of the 'everlasting covenant' announced in 61:8 are elucidated further with the note of righteousness to the fore—verse 1, 'For Zion's sake I will not keep silent, and for

85

Jerusalem's sake I will not be quiet, until her righteousness goes forth as brightness, and her salvation as a burning torch.' All of this fulfils the eschatological vision laid out in chapter 2 of Isaiah, 'in the latter days ... the mountain of the house of the Lord shall be established as the highest of the mountains, and shall be lifted up above the hills; and all the nations shall flow to it, and many peoples shall come, and say: "Come, let us go up to the mountain of the Lord, to the house of the God of Jacob, that he may teach us his ways and that we may walk in his paths." For out of Zion shall go the law, and the word of the Lord from Jerusalem'

Isaiah is the only prophet who uses the light metaphor to any significant extent. The link between God's presence, the change this occasions amongst his people and his salvific purposes for the world, is a close one. Alec Motyer commenting on Isaiah 60 writes: 'When the Redeemer has come to Zion, gathered his penitents (59:20) and appointed a covenant mediator to share the Lord's Spirit with them, it is not just that they are bathed in light but that they are irradiated, inwardly charged with new, outshining life ... This subjective experience has an objective basis, *for your light has come.*'[1]

Furthermore, the presence of God as symbolised by the light metaphor and its saving and transforming witnessing effect, are also closely associated with the theme of 'righteousness' which is dominant in chapter 62 and the work of God's 'Anointed One'— the Messiah. The work of this divine agent which has been set forth in chapter 61 is to bring about a new status of righteousness before God, a rescue from bondage (verse 1) and a visible righteousness of life (verse 2).[2]

Thus, the flow of the revelation in this section is the elevation of a New Jerusalem, the formation of a people of righteousness who will become a light to the nations. It will be a time of unprecedented covenant fidelity resulting in an inward movement of peoples drawn to the light and an outward movement of God's word/law.

All of this has direct bearing on our key section and, in turn, our understanding of the relation between Gospel proclamation and social involvement.

Jesus speaking to his disciples (the 'poor'—afflicted ones who engage in prophetic ministry), is emphatic: '*You are* the salt of the earth; *you are* the light of the world.' Here we discover a correspondence with the structure of the beatitudes themselves:— the first four describing the condition of the members of the kingdom, the second four relating their activity. In other words, their 'doing'—showing mercy, godliness (pure in heart); peacemaking and a prophetic ministry of righteousness—arising out of their 'being'—followers of Christ. This is also very much in line with what we have just been discussing regarding the Zion of the last days. It is because of the salvation experienced through God's servant that not only has a new status of righteousness been bestowed, but a new life of righteousness is being lived.

The sense and referent of the metaphors

We now turn to examine a little more closely what is meant by the two metaphors salt and light and consider their connection with the third metaphor, a 'city on a hill.'

First, the description of the disciples as the 'salt of the earth.'

Given the substantiated premise that Isaiah 40–66 stands behind the Sermon on the Mount, it is perhaps suggestive that the Servant of the Lord in Isaiah 42:6 is described as one who is sent 'as a covenant for the people, a light for the nations, to open the eyes that are blind' On the basis of the covenant renewal, the light goes forth to the ends of the earth. This was to be the task of Israel as symbolised by Mount Zion in Isaiah 2, a servant which failed and which became blind and deaf (Isaiah 42:18) and so being as much in need as the Gentiles. This task has now been fulfilled by Jesus (Matthew 5:17ff) and, in turn, his gathered community. If the parallel is to be maintained it follows that being the 'salt of the earth' is a symbolic reference to *maintaining the covenant*.

This is an interpretation which is justified by a consideration of the Old Testament use of 'salt' in covenantal agreements, e.g. Leviticus 2:13: 'season all your grain offerings with salt. You shall not let the *salt of the covenant* with your God be missing from your grain offering; with all your offerings you shall offer salt.'; 2 Chronicles 13:5: 'Ought you not to know that the LORD God of

Israel gave the kingship over Israel forever to David and his sons by a covenant of salt?' Could not the way the metaphor functions be that just as salt has the quality of making something last which would otherwise decay—having a preserving quality—so there is a concern to preserve the covenant, thus making it last when otherwise it would not? When this metaphor is transferred to the work of the prophets we readily see how it would operate. The task of the prophetic ministry is to remind the people of the covenant and the way of life which is consistent with that covenant and ensuring its continuing operation. In this way the prophets acted as 'salt of the covenant', seeking to maintain the covenant's integrity amongst God's people.

For the disciples to fulfil *their* duty of being the salt of the earth (salt of the land?), they, like the prophets, have to remain distinctive and speak God's truth. *Prima facie,* therefore, if a strict parallel is to be maintained, it could be argued that it is a *proclamatory* ministry which is being envisaged here as was the case with the OT prophets. [3] Acting in a salt-like capacity involves calling people to be true to the way of life of the new covenant community, a way of life Jesus expounds in the rest of the Sermon. Such a ministry will invariably meet with resistance as Jesus has just warned. It is when faced with such opposition that his followers run the danger of losing their saltiness either by adopting values and lifestyles indistinct from the people being addressed and/or by diluting the message being brought to bear and so in effect becoming a false prophet (Matthew 7:15ff). If this happens, as it did with Israel herself, there will be a 'trampling under foot' in judgement (cf. Isaiah 5:5; 10:6; 22:5). The salt metaphor then, has little to do with 'penetrating society' and so 'preserving' it. It has much more to do with the followers of Jesus engaging in a 'prophetic' word ministry which brings people into covenant relationship with the one true God through Jesus Christ which in turn leads to change of values and lives which flow from that covenant. [4]

We now move on to the second metaphor, 'the light of the world' which is specifically linked to the 'city on a hill which cannot be hidden.' (verse 14).

In Isaiah it is Zion which is to be such a city, the community of the redeemed whose light and shining righteousness attracts the nations in the end times (60:1–3; 62:1–3). The 'irradiated' 'inwardly charged, new life' which shines like a light, referred to by Motyer, is, according to the prophets Ezekiel and Jeremiah, brought about by the pouring out of God's Spirit and the bestowal of new hearts on which are written God's law (Ezekiel 36:24–32; Jeremiah 31:31–34). But it would appear that Jesus is giving the symbols of light and a city a new referent, namely, the poor/prophetic community of his followers. In Isaiah 62:2, the nations (Gentiles) will see the righteousness of the redeemed which shines out of them 'as a burning torch', likewise, this new 'city' of the redeemed cannot be hid and their righteous good works (which are to exceed those of the Pharisees), will be seen and result in the offering of praise to God the Father (v 16). It is by being salt within one's own circle—calling God's people to be true to his covenant and being true to it oneself—that the covenant community will influence the world by drawing others to the one true God. It is also from this community that God's law/word goes into the world as a source of blessing (cf. Isaiah 2:3). This is the *raison d'être* of the community: just as a lamp placed on a stand is to illumine the whole house, (a hidden lamp defeating its purpose) so there can be no retreat *from* the world for these Kingdom people if they are to be a light *to* the world. It is 'before men' that such deeds are performed and so producing a desired doxological effect (5:16).

It is not without significance that the same programmatic pattern established here at the beginning of his Gospel is repeated by Matthew at the end of the Gospel in chapter 28:16ff. On that mountain the Son of Man, who has received all authority and an everlasting kingdom (cf. Daniel 7:13), gathers his people in order to disperse them into the world with the specified task of proclaiming and demonstrating his rule. This involves making disciples of all people groups, baptising them into his teaching [5] so that they will obey all that has been commanded (cf. Matthew 5:19). This is the calling of his people which they are to maintain until the end of the age when the reign of God which has been inaugurated will be consummated. What is anticipated and promised in Isaiah—a new heavens and new earth (66:22)—will finally be realised at the end of time. It is the renewed covenant community, the city on a hill, which is God's chosen vehicle for achieving these things.

David Seccombe expresses well the relationship between the Servant, his gathered people and their mission:

> At the time of the Sermon on the Mount Jesus evidently did not see himself carrying out the Servant's mission as an isolated individual. We observe, how, having declared the gospel, he appeals to all who have ears to hear. This is a plea for response, and the nature of that response is to become his disciple and join him in his mission of suffering; he warns them that if they will not they will never see his kingdom. This is because first, the role of the Suffering Servant was Israel's role; secondly only in default did the task pass on to the disciples, and finally with their defection, to one individual. Thus Jesus calls upon all who heard him to join him in an active programme of outgoing love and generosity that would engage with others and demonstrate God's goodness. It would meet opposition with generosity, prayer, and a willingness to suffer. God was seeking to be reconciled with his enemies, and his sons were called to participate in the peacemaking initiative (Luke 6:27–38).[6]

The co-ordination of evangelism and social action

We are now in a position to see more clearly how evangelism and social action are to be co-ordinated, arising out of, and modelled by, the Sermon on the Mount and shaped by the Isaianic motifs which lie behind it.

First, there is the heralding of the good news, the *euangelion*. The blessings themselves are evangelistic, declaring the good news of the year of the Lord's favour to his afflicted people—the *ptochoi*— that the kingdom is theirs.[7] As the word of the Lord was to go out from Mount Zion in Isaiah's oracle, it now goes out from the 'new city on a hill' as represented here by Jesus' disciples. Evangelism is the priority ministry so that all nations will receive the blessing promised to Abraham (Genesis 12), hearing the news that there is now an appointed ruler of the house of David (2 Samuel 7) and his name is Jesus who is the Christ (Matthew 1:1). The time of Exile is now over, God has come to dwell amongst his people in the form of the one who is called 'Emmanuel' (Isaiah 7:14; Matthew 1:23). As the suffering Servant, he atones for the sins of his people (Matthew 1:21/Isaiah 52:13–53:12). What was said of *the* Servant—singular can also be said of his servants—plural: 'How beautiful upon the mountains are the feet of him who brings good news, who publishes peace, who brings good news of happiness, who publishes salvation, who says to Zion, "Your God reigns"' (Isaiah 52:7/Romans 10:15).[8] Furthermore, given the cataclysmic nature of *not* responding to this message (Matthew 7:13, 23, 27) the urgency as well as the priority of Gospel proclamation is underscored.

Secondly, as salt, the followers of Jesus are to engage in a prophetic ministry and so ensure that the new covenant remains operative. Here again the priority is word ministry—declaring to people Gospel truths. But these truths are not to be understood in a reductionist fashion, they embrace the concerns for justice and right living that God has. Social relations lie at the heart of Jesus' prophetic application of the law (Matthew 5:21–7:12) as they did for Isaiah himself (Isaiah 1; 2:6ff; 5:8ff *passim*). At the centre of the great 'Jubilee' passage of Isaiah 61 we find these words: 'For I the Lord love justice; I hate robbery and wrong' (v8). If his followers are to be faithful to their calling as 'prophetic salt' in maintaining the integrity of the covenant, can they settle for anything less? Such ministry is costly and it is often from the professing religious people that opposition will most likely come (as Jesus and the apostles were soon to discover).

Thirdly, as a community of light, God's people are to embody and express the new life of the kingdom amongst themselves and outwards to others: being as prodigal in loving forgiveness as God is himself (Matthew 5:44); giving generously to those in need (6:1ff); refusing to serve Mammon and instead storing up treasures in heaven (6:19ff); learning contentment and eschewing judgementalism (7:1ff). This is a community of light which will shine; whose deeds will impact upon a watching world and act as a witness to the reality of the breaking in of God's kingdom here on earth.

To test whether this thesis is sound, we turn to the life and activity of the early church as recorded in the Book of Acts.

ENDNOTES

1. A. Motyer, *The Prophecy of Isaiah* (Leicester: IVP, 1993), p. 494

2. Ibid p. 506.

3. Since this Sermon constitutes the platform for Jesus ministry in Matthew, with Jesus gathering his disciples to prepare them as his followers, and given the centrality of preaching in his own ministry (Mark 1:38), it would be most extraordinary to say the least, if *no* instruction were offered by Jesus on the proclamatory aspects of ministry. What is more, one of the main characteristics of the Servant in Isaiah is that he is one who *proclaims* God's Word (Isaiah 49:1, 2, 52:7, 53:1, 61:1-2). This interpretation of the disciples being salt fills what would otherwise be an astonishing lacunae in the Sermon.

4. The apostle Paul may be using the metaphor of salt in this way in Colossians 4:6, 'Let your speech always be gracious, seasoned with salt, so that you may know how you ought to answer each person.' The content of this 'conversation' is 'the mystery of Christ' (verse 2), which is why he is in chains and asks for prayers so he can proclaim it clearly (verse 3). Here then, in the life of Paul, is another example of the prophetic-word salt ministry and one which results in persecution.

5. D. B. Knox presents a very strong case that this is the correct understanding of the use of 'baptism' in Matthew 28 in his chapter 'New Testament Baptism' in *D. B. Knox Collected Works, Volume* 11 (Matthias Media, 2002). He concludes: 'The 'great commission' of Jesus contains no reference to administering water baptism. The reference to baptizing is entirely metaphorical in line with other uses of the word by Jesus. It is a command to proclaim the news of the Messiah's coming to the nations to make them disciples of the true God, to immerse the nations into the revealed character of God so that their whole way of life is changed and their cultures sanctified (cf. Revelation 21:26).' p. 278.

6. Op cit. p. 259. Similarly David Peterson writes of Jesus' ethic as presented in the Sermon on the Mount, 'It is an ethic for the community of disciples, called to live for Jesus in a special relationship with one another and with a hostile world, holding forth to the world the message of the kingdom and living out the values and attitudes of the kingdom in anticipation of its consummation by God at the end of human history. Jesus does not provide a pattern for transforming society per se, but intends that the lifestyle of the disciples individually and collectively should be both judgement on fallen humanity and a pointer to the possibility of renewal and change under the rule of God.' 'Jesus and Social Ethics' in *'Christians and Society'* Barry Webb (ed), p. 92 (Lancer, 1988).

7. Those who have argued at length for the evangelistic character of the beatitudes are reviewed by Seccombe in his *Possessions,* pp. 34f, 85f.

8. Note the priority of proclaiming God's truth 'justice' in the first servant song. Motyer writes: 'Justice is the leading idea in this first Servant Song, pointing to the scope of the servant's work, his reliability in its discharge and his perseverance through to its accomplishment. The word '*mishpaṭ*' is versatile, but its sense is plain in this context... It is a summary word for his revealed truth (cf. in verse 4, the parallelism between justice and law/'teaching') and its requirements. In this wide sense the servant brings the truth of God to the world, a pointed contrast to their former situation.' Op cit. p. 319.

8

What it means to be 'Salt, Light and a City on a Hill' in the Book of Acts

The Priority of Proclamation

I have argued that although the two metaphors of salt and light are related they are nonetheless distinct; being salt and engaging in prophetic action is a necessary condition for being light and vice versa. This distinction is maintained in the Book of Acts in relation to the proclamatory, evangelistic work of the apostles and the communal life of the Christian believers. This dichotomy also has bearing on the question as to whether it can legitimately be claimed that the church *qua* church actually has a 'mission'.

Private and Public

Brad Blue[1] has shown that a clear differentiation of activities occurs in Acts between those which took place within the confines of a private domestic residence (the house church) and those which required a more open, public setting: 'Luke consistently pairs the public and private activities of the early church. On the one hand, the Temple precincts, synagogues, lecture halls, etc. served as platforms from which to preach the gospel. On the other, the converted hearers formed a community centred in the houses which were placed at the communities' disposal by affluent Christians.'[2]

In turning to Acts 5:42, he argues that the chiastic (cross-like structure) construction suggests the activity of the house churches was distinct from the public proclamation which took place in the Temple precincts: 'Every day, in the temple and from house to house, they did not cease teaching and preaching that the Christ is Jesus.' A parallel construction and so a similar distinction is found in Acts 20:20; 'I did not shrink from declaring to you anything that was profitable, and teaching you in public and from house to house.' Also, the reference in Acts 5:21 to the apostles entering the Temple courts and beginning to teach is no exception. This is just another way of saying that they proclaimed the Gospel since the command of the angel in v. 20 who released them from prison, was to 'Go and stand in the temple and speak to the people all the words of this Life' (13:26; in Syriac 'life' and 'salvation' are rendered by the same word). Marshall goes on to say, 'The use of this word is odd (cf. 22:4), but is perhaps a Lucan trick of style.' [3]

This interpretation [4] could be applied to unravel the summary description of the activities of the early Christians in Acts 2:46:

Day after day	
They steadfastly met together in the temple Place (public)	In their houses breaking bread Place (private)
Sharing food with glad and generous hearts. Main clause: characteristic of private gatherings.	
Praising God Place (private)	Having goodwill towards all the people (Echontes charin pros holon ton laon) Place (public)
The Lord added to their number those being saved Main clause: results of the public activity Day after day	

Blue concludes: 'If we have rightly understood the Lucan presentation of early Christianity, both in Palestine and the Greco-Roman world, the gospel was first proclaimed in the publicly acceptable places. Subsequently, those who had responded were drawn together into house gatherings. Luke never even suggests that during these private meetings of believers the gospel message was preached for the purpose of converting the hearers. On the contrary, for Luke, these private house meetings were for the benefit of the Christian community alone.' [5]

It is being proposed here that this pattern of public proclamation and private gathering parallels the two functions of being salt and light.

First, there is the ministry of the word in evangelism. On the day of Pentecost the redeemed community is gathered in an upper room (Acts 1:13). With the pouring out of the Holy Spirit by the Messiah the scene shifts as the group spills out into the public arena, the most natural setting being the Temple precincts which at that time of day would have been busy. It is here that Jesus is declared Lord and Christ, fulfilling the promise of Scripture (2:32). In response to the preaching of Peter, the people are called to repent and be baptised in the name of Jesus. The setting is Jerusalem—Mount Zion. The people are being called to a renewed covenant relation with God as evidence by the giving of the Spirit (Joel 2:28ff; Ezekiel 36:24ff). The gathering in of God's people to Zion has started from the Diaspora as represented by the different language groups present (2:9ff). This continued on a daily basis (2:47; 3:1; 5:12ff). The everlasting covenant made to David is fulfilled in Jesus and offered to the people (3:24–26).

Not surprisingly, given Jesus' warning in Matthew 5:11, such 'salt activity' is soon met with opposition from the ruling authorities (Acts 4:1ff; 5:17–40). Whilst the occasion for the harassment and arrest of the apostles in Acts 4 is the healing of the crippled beggar, the focus of concern for the Sanhedrin was the 'name' by which the miracle took place. As David Peterson has shown, this represents the divine authority and continued blessings of Jesus in salvation. Accordingly, it is the content of the Gospel proclaimed which is the underlying issue and cause of contention rather than the 'act of kindness' itself (4:9). Peter well understands this and it forms the basis of his defence (4:10ff). This view is also borne out by the subsequent arrest and miraculous release recorded in chapter 5 when the apostles are forbidden to *teach* 'in this name'. (5:28).[6]

It was for 'acts of righteousness' that they suffer and, accordingly, they take Jesus' injunction literally when having foretold of persecution because of him they are to 'rejoice and be glad' (Acts 5:41).[7]

But the prophetic activity was also directed inwards to the redeemed community, the 'city on a hill'. This comes out most clearly in the Ananias and Sapphira episode (Acts 5:1–11). Their lying to the Holy Spirit was met with swift and deadly judgement such that 'great fear came upon the whole church and upon all who heard of these things' (5:11). The words of Peter are reminiscent of the words of the Old Testament prophets to Israel.[8] Such behaviour was a denial of the new covenant and the renewed life which flows from it and as such threatened its future existence.

All of this is matched by the 'light' motif. As the redeemed community, new values and generous lifestyles were to be adopted and expressed. For Luke it is the formation of a community of property which most markedly reflects these things as indicated by its repetition in his first two summaries: Acts 2:44–45 and 4:32, 34. The statement of the last verse that, 'there were no needy (*endees*) among them', suggests the fulfilling of the Mosaic law of Deuteronomy 15:4.[9] Although the language may be verging on the overstatement, Brian Capper provides some insight into the significance of what Luke records when he writes: 'Luke's intent is salvation-historical as well as ethical. As a salvation-historical reference, his account draws out the momentous significance of God's new act of the creation of the Church. God's Spirit of love, poured out on the community of his Messiah, brings a new ethical creation characterised by the koinonia which the first uncorrupted human beings shared. That a new phase of history has begun is symbolised by the momentary return of a paradisal state of the first human beings. Since the eschatological hope is hope for a return to paradise, Luke's description is also a glimpse of the eschatological future. The story of the Church's beginnings reveals its true essence as the vehicle of eschatological salvation through which all creation will be renewed.'[10] More modestly

I would suggest what is envisaged is a reversal of the corrupt Zion which Isaiah condemned and the inauguration of the eschatological community he foresaw. Instead of joining 'house to house' and adding 'field to field' in greed (Isaiah 5:8) houses and fields were sold in order to meet need (Acts 4:34). Whereas in former Jerusalem the cause of the widows was neglected (Isaiah 1:23), in God's new Zion it is met (Acts 6:1ff). [11]

Although the public and private activities of the early church can be distinguished, the distinction is not a hard and fast one. It is highly unlikely that others in Jerusalem were unaware of the activities of the church in caring and sharing. What is more, the word ministry of the apostles to the people was accompanied by a ministry of healing miracles (Acts 5:12–16). Both would clearly constitute the 'good works' spoken of by Jesus and mirror the pattern of his own ministry (Matthew 4:23ff).

Does the *Church* have a 'mission'?

In the debate on the relation between evangelism and social action, both are often bracketed together as at least being different but complementary aspects of the Church's 'mission'. In recent years the suitability of this phrase as applied to the church has been brought into question.

Here is Peter Bolt: 'The concept of the "mission of the church" ought to be laid to rest. Acts does not present "the Church" as an institution which is sent. A particular church may send individuals to do a particular work (cf.13:1–4), but the church itself is not sent.' [12] Similarly John Woodhouse comments, 'The New Testament does not contain this concept. The apostles are "sent". And one may suppose that evangelists are "sent". Perhaps in some sense all Christians are "sent" (John 20:21). But the "church" as the church is not "sent". Individuals are given *to* the church, "sent" to the church if you like (Ephesians 4:11) and the church sends individuals (Acts 13:3). But we do not find the *church* with a mission. This is because the New Testament concept of "church" is not of an institution. All the "sending" has the gathering of God's people by the gospel as its goal. The gathering, the "church", is not the means to some other goal.' [13]

This is very much in accord with what we have already seen in Acts. The public proclamation of the gospel has as its *goal* the addition of people to the gathering/church (Acts 2:47). This is where they receive the apostles' teaching and experience fellowship as the redeemed community thus actualising in some measure the Zion of the last days spoken of by Isaiah with 'nations coming to your light' (Isaiah 60:3) and being 'taught his ways' (Isaiah 2:3). Individuals or groups of individuals are 'sent out' (as were the disciples in Matthew 10) but with a view to 'gathering in' (Acts 5:12–14). The priority of Word ministry is asserted by the apostles in Acts 6:2 in response to the pending crisis amongst the Grecian Jewish widows that, 'It is not right that we should give up preaching the word of God to serve tables', but nonetheless practical steps are taken so as not to neglect the needy provision of widows which would have undermined the ministry in a different way, for by denying the proper expression of the new covenant the salt would be in danger of losing its saltiness.

Summary

The early church took seriously Jesus' command to be 'salt and light', understood correctly against its Old Testament background. As 'salt' they followed the tradition of the prophets in proclaiming God's covenant as now fulfilled in Christ and lived out by his new kingdom communities. As 'light' they displayed their 'deeds of righteousness' and so corporately acted like 'cities on hills', distinctive from their pagan surroundings. Here belief and behaviour, declaration and deed were fully integrated.

ENDNOTES

1. Brad Blue, 'The Influence of Jewish Worship on Luke's Presentation of the Early Church', in *Witness to the Gospel, The Theology of Acts*, (I. H. Marshall and D. Peterson, eds.), (Grand Rapids: Eerdmans, 1998).

2. Ibid p. 482

3. I. H. Marshall, *Acts* (Leicester: IVP, 1980) p. 118.

4. Originally proposed by Klauck and cited by Blue, p. 486

5. Ibid. p. 486

6. See D. Peterson, 'Worship in the New Community' in *Witness to the Gospel*, p. 381.

7. The most striking example in Acts of the exercise of prophetic ministry of which Jesus speaks and the consequent opposition is Stephen in Acts 6 and 7. Note how in true prophetic style he recalls the history of Israel, the peoples' habitual covenant breaking and the persecution of the prophets of which the rejection of Jesus forms the climax (7:51–53).

8. See Isaiah 66:2b-4

9. Deuteronomy 15: 4, 'However, there should be no poor among you ...' the LXX uses *endees*.

10. Brian Capper, 'Reciprocity and the Ethic of Acts' in *Witness to the Gospel*, p. 511.

11. Capper argues that 'Although Luke describes the community of goods of Acts 2–6 with remarkable enthusiasm, the later chapters of Acts do not suggest that he wished his readers to institute formal property sharing arrangements. Rather, his model becomes almsgiving.' Ibid p. 499.

12. Peter Bolt, 'Mission and Witness' in *Witness to the Gospel*, p. 211.

13. John Woodhouse 'Evangelism and Social Responsibility' B. G. Webb (ed) *Christians in Society* Exploration 3 (Lancer 1998) p. 22. The position of Bolt and Woodhouse has been checked and qualified by Dr Mark Thompson as he points out that solely focusing on the word 'ekklesia' can lead to distorted thinking regarding mission, for other concepts are also used to describe God's people other than that of 'gathering.' He writes, 'The gospel mission is always first and foremost God's mission. Nevertheless the broad sweep of biblical theology indicates that those God has redeemed are involved in the advance of the redemptive work of God. that this applies to the redeemed whether gathered in "church" or scattered in the world is evident from the constancy of the redemptive relationship.' 'Does the Local church have a Mission? In *Exploring the Missionary Church* (Explorations 7, Lancer, Ed B.G. Webb, 1993)

9

Getting Personal and Practical

Evangelism and Social Action in
'Reaching the unreached'

Introduction

How do the principles explored in the previous chapters concerning the relationship between evangelism and social action work out in practice? This is the question we shall be exploring in this final chapter. Obviously, it will largely be practical but this does not mean being simply pragmatic. To use a contemporary phrase, what follows is 'principled pragmatism.'

All theology is done within a personal context. This is not to say that the personal determines the content of one's theology—that privileged position belongs to the Bible alone—but rather that what we reflect upon theologically and excites us, is to a larger or lesser extent influenced by our past background and present concerns.

One of the great challenges facing evangelicalism in the UK is the 'reaching of the unreached'. This is the way Tim Chester describes the present situation: 'Research conducted by Tearfund in 2007 shows that churchgoing in the UK is a middle-class pursuit. Adults in social grades AB (professionals, senior and middle management) are over-represented among both regular and occasional churchgoers. Meanwhile, adults of social grade C2 and D (skilled, semi-skilled and manual) have the highest proportion of non-churched. Julian Rebera from new Life Church in Brighton concludes, "There are very few churches on deprived estates. Those that exist are not attended by people from the estates, but by people outside the estates. And very few people from the estates travel out to our city-centre, largely white middle-class churches."[1]

It is the challenge of reaching 'the unreached' in our cities and urban towns with the Gospel, not just the traditional 'working class', but now many other people groups including those from Eastern Europe and asylum seekers, which underscores the urgency of getting the relationship between evangelism and social action right in both theory and practice.

Getting Personal

Let me share something of my own background which explains my own concern to reach the unreached.

The fact is—I was one of them.

My background is thoroughly working class.

I was brought up in a coal mining town in Nottinghamshire in the 1960s. This was D. H. Lawrence country—'Sons and Lovers' and all that! My Dad was a coal miner and my maternal grandfather was also a miner before leaving the pit to work at the local sewage plant. I lived on one of the roughest streets in our town. One example will suffice to illustrate just how rough it was. Once as our family were sitting down for an evening of telly watching, a brick came hurtling through the window!

I attended one of the very first comprehensive schools, built as a flagship school in 1964. I remember that in my third year pretty well never a week went by without me being involved in a fist fight behind the bike sheds. What is more, I was expected to leave school at 15 to earn money since further education was considered to be something 'we didn't do'. Had it not been for the encouragement of my teachers I wouldn't have gone against my Dad's wishes to leave school and join the army, but instead I stayed on to take 'O' and 'A' levels and then to do the unthinkable—attend university!

As a family we had no time for church or Christianity and on the whole we were antagonistic to both, although, (as I will mention again later) there was some warmth and respect towards the

Salvation Army. How, then did I become a Christian? The answer: through personal contact with a Christian family. The significance of this to our subject will become apparent in a moment.

Not a new problem

It is important to point out that that contrary to the popular perception, even the early church was *not* a movement of the 'marginalised and dispossessed'. The popular view came about in a variety of ways. One of its early proponents was Friedrich Engels (the friend of Karl Marx) who wrote, 'Christianity was originally a movement of oppressed people: it first appeared as the religion of slaves and emancipated slaves, of poor people deprived of all rights, of peoples subjugated or dispersed by Rome.'[2] Probably one of the first major scholars to question the 'proletariat thesis' accounting for the rise of Christianity, was E. A. Judge in 1960 who, after a careful analysis of the ranks and occupations mentioned in the early sources, concluded, 'Far from being a socially depressed group ... the Christians were dominated by a socially pretentious section of the population of big cities. Beyond that they seem to have drawn on a broad constituency, probably representing the household dependents of leading members.'[3] More recently this has been placed on firmer footing by sociologist, Professor Rodney Stark who has undertaken a detailed numerical and statistical analysis of the rise of Christianity.[4] He has shown that Christianity tended to be stronger in the cities than in the country and that the very word *pagan* points to this fact—*paganus*—meaning 'countrymen' or 'rural dwellers' which later came to refer to non-Christians.

Stark has shown that cults tend to attract affluent, thinking people (see Table 1). When applied to early Christianity, Stark argues that we see the same pattern emerging as it began as a cult within Judaism. His conclusion is that cult movements over-recruit persons of more privileged backgrounds (by cult he means religious groups which show a high degree of tension with the surrounding culture—i.e. they are radically different). Those evangelical churches which are being influential in rich, university towns simply illustrate what is to be expected on the basis of this analysis. From a sociological point of view it is easier to grow such churches. However, as we shall see, this does not mean that over time the early church didn't penetrate the lower classes and win converts, they did. In fact the growth was phenomenal as we see from Table 2:

Percent Who Attended College	
DENOMINATION	
Presbyterian	61%
Methodist	46%
Lutheran	45%
CULTS	
New Age	67%
Scientology	81%
Wiccan	83%
Eckankar	90%
Deity	100%

Table 1

Christian Growth Projected at 40% per Decade

Year	Number of Christians	Percent of Population
40	1,000	0.0017
50	1,400	0.0023
100	7,530	0.0126
150	40,496	0.07
200	217,795	0.36
250	1,171,356	1.9
300	6,299,832	10.5
350	33,882,008	56.5

Table 2

Based on an estimated population of 60 million

Working on the rate of growth at 40% per decade or 3.4% a year we see that by the year 350 AD over half the Roman Empire would have had some allegiance to the Christian faith. It is an exponential growth and this is not so far-fetched as it might first appear because this is precisely the rate of growth of Mormonism.

Networks and making connections

How did (and does), this kind of growth take place, (allowing for prayer and the sovereign work of God's Spirit as well as the vital factor of biological growth as Christians tended to have more children than the pagans)? This is where the principle we see being worked out by the apostle Paul in 1 Corinthians 9:19–23 comes into play, 'For though I am free from all, I have made myself a servant to all, that I might win more of them. To the Jews I became as a Jew, in order to win Jews. To those under the law I became as one under the law (though not being myself under the law) that I might win those under the law. To those outside the law I became as one outside the law (not being outside the law of God but under the law of Christ) that I might win those outside the law. To the weak I became weak, that I might win the weak. I have become all things to all people, that by all means I might save some. I do it all for the sake of the gospel, that I may share with them in its blessings.'

This is quite a complex argument as D. A. Carson has demonstrated,[5] but the basic principle is clear: Paul wishes to adopt the posture of a servant, and so imitate Christ (1 Corinthians 11:1) in that he is willing to sacrifice certain of his own rights and, we might add, personal preferences, so as to minimise the distance between himself and those he is trying to reach in order to 'save some'. Thus he is willing to show a fair degree of flexibility to this end, becoming like a Jew to Jews and a Gentile to Gentiles. But this is not a free floating flexibility as it is shaped and motivated by faithfulness to the Gospel of which proclamation is primary (vv. 16–18). In other words, central to reaching out is making *connections* with those we are trying to reach and doing so in ways which are appropriate and meaningful. Barriers are reduced to a minimum and bridges are extended to a maximum.

Getting from 'here' to 'there'

One of the most effective means of making connections is through *social networks*. Let's take a non-Christian example—the Unification church or as they are commonly referred to—the Moonies. Again, Stark provides some helpful insights.[6]

In the early 1960s Stark and Lofland decided to actually go out and *watch* how people converted to this group. A Korean Moonie, Dr Kim arrived in San Francisco in 1959 with a small group of converts from Oregon. At first she tried to spread her message directly through talks to various groups, radio slots, press releases and the like. All of this amounted to nothing. But as time passed it was observed *how* people were converted. The first few converts were old friends or relatives of members who came from Oregon for a visit. Subsequent converts were people who formed close friendships with one or more members of the group. The social networks enabled people to see faith in action first-hand as it were—and so made the faith plausible. It was striking that pretty well all the converts had no prior religious commitment. Of further interest are the results of the interviews with folk as to why they converted. The conclusion was that, 'Converts very seldom are religious seeker—most converts do not so much find a new faith as the new faith finds them.'[7] They also showed that doctrine only plays a *secondary* role when people *initially* make their choices. Starke and Finke don't deny for a moment that doctrine is important; in fact it is vital for both generating and sustaining commitment—i.e. believing things to be *true*. But in the *first instance* what is of primary significance is coming into contact with members, being attracted by what they do and becoming more attached to group members than non-group members and finding out what makes them tick which includes what they believe.[8]

Obviously the Unification Church is a sect and displays cult-like features and is as far removed from Christianity as one can possibly be—*theologically* they are way off beam, but *sociologically* they do serve as a useful illustration of a more general principle: the importance of focusing on *people* and displaying a difference in the context of social networks.

As I have already indicated, this was my experience.

As an older teenager I wasn't particularly looking for answers to the meaning of life. I was quite happy enjoying life! I would never have given a moment's thought to setting foot inside a church building. Why should I (apart for a wedding or a funeral of course)? However, I did come into contact with a Christian family and over a long period of time as they befriended me and talked openly about things, I became convinced and so became converted.

In part, the phenomenal growth of Christianity in the first four centuries which did get to embrace peoples of the lower classes is a result of such networking. How were such connections made? 'Christianity served as a revitalization movement that arose in response to the misery, chaos, fear and brutality of life in the urban Greco-Roman world.' That it 'revitalized life in Greco-Roman cities by providing new norms and kinds of social relationships able to cope with many urgent urban problems. To cities filled with the homeless and impoverished, Christianity offered charity as well as hope. To cities filled with newcomers and strangers, Christianity offered an immediate basis for attachments. To cities filled with orphans and widows, Christianity provided a new and expanded sense of family. To cities torn by violent ethnic strife, Christianity offered a new basis for social solidarity. And to cities faced with epidemics, fires and earthquakes, Christianity offered effective nursing services.'[9]

Let us take the latter example of the offer of nursing by the early Christians.

In 260 AD, during what was probably a massive measles epidemic, Dionysius Bishop of Alexandria wrote: 'Most of our brother Christians showed unbounded love and loyalty, never sparing themselves and thinking only of one another. Heedless of the danger; they took charge of the sick, attending every need and ministering to them in Christ, and with them departed this life serenely happy; for they were infected by others with the disease, drawing on themselves the sickness of their neighbours and cheerfully accepting their pains.. Many, in nursing and curing others, transferred death to themselves and died in their stead ... The best of our brothers lost their lives in this manner, a number of presbyters, deacons, and laymen winning high commendation so that death in this form, the result of great piety and strong faith, seems in every way the equal of martyrdom.'[10] Contrast this with a description of the way the pagans were operating: 'The heathen behaved in the very opposite way. At the first onset of the disease, they pushed the sufferers away and fled from their dearest, throwing them into the roads before they were dead and treated unburied corpses as dirt, hoping thereby to avert the spread and contagion of the fatal disease; but do what they might, they found it difficult to escape.' That this was not the hyperbolic licence of a preacher, casting the 'opposition' in a bad light, is substantiated by a similar description of the activity of non-Christians in Athens by Thucydides in 431 BC.[11] The contrast with the care offered by Christians was something which caused the Emperor 'Julian the Apostate' great consternation in 362 as he complained, 'The impious Galileans support not only their poor, but ours as well, everyone can see that our people lack aid from us.' [12]

Here we are given a clear indication of one of the ways the early church made a significant impact upon its surrounding culture as word and deed worked themselves out in an unsophisticated and almost unselfconscious way. It is not that we are to have two separate intentions—providing social care on the one hand and engaging in evangelism on the other. Or that the *real* aim is to evangelise and the social action is just a subsidiary means towards that end. The two can be represented in terms of double intention so that Christians want to help people who are in need socially *and* evangelise and *both* can be achieved through the same and similarly related activities.

One of our major problems facing the church today in the UK is the lack of Christian presence amongst the working classes, whether urban or rural so there are little no meaningful connections being made. What is more, the distance that we have creates the impression that not only do we not care but also that we are an irrelevance. This cuts right across Paul's principle of 1 Corinthians 9. So how are networks to be formed?

Let me draw on our experience at St Johns, Newland in Hull.

St Johns stands next to one of the most densely populated and deprived areas of the city. Unemployment in Hull is around 12%. Over 50% of the people do not have a car. Just 5% are in professional/managerial work. Home ownership is very low. The city has a high rate of mortality from all causes. It also has the lowest church attendance in the country hovering around 0.6%.

St John's itself has a real mix of folk, including many from working class backgrounds—and by that I don't mean low paid or manual workers, (though we have those) but folk who may own their own homes but whose values and outlook are not middle or upper class. If you want to see how finely nuanced those are, then read Kate Fox's *'Watching the English.'* [13] We have a strong mix of ages and increasingly people from different ethnic backgrounds.

How have many of these been contacted?

First, we have a Christian primary school, as well as being involved in a state primary school and a good number of families have come through this route. We have been able to develop after-school groups at both schools. We also set up a Christian nursery which is run on distinctly Christian lines with Christian staff. This has been especially fruitful in making connections with non-Christian families. The whole of one such family came to faith because one of their daughters was coming home from school asking questions about Jesus and they thought they ought to start coming to church to find out. The Mum was converted first and then the Dad. This has happened on several occasions. We have also developed links through setting up parents and toddler groups, music sessions for toddlers and their Mums, and a fortnightly Saturday morning session for Dads and young children who are keen on football, called 'Kick-it'. This has proved very popular with non-Christian fathers especially.

Secondly, we have been developing what we call 'Community Action' and have employed a community action minister to head this up. In assessing the value of a particular work, three criteria have been adopted. First, there is the assessment that the work in itself will be of benefit to our 'neighbour'. Real needs are to be met. Secondly, there is the intention of bringing people into contact with members of the church family through the work so that in some measure they can 'taste and see' the community of the Kingdom. Thirdly, there is the desire and intention to verbally share the Gospel. Obviously, there are always more demands than can be met and so value judgements have to be made as to which work will be given priority in terms of time and resources. But the Gospel lies at the heart of it all in terms of the motivation and theological grounding as unpacked in this book, as well as the priority of proclaiming the Gospel message.

There are two areas especially where we have sought to engage in Gospel ministry in terms of community action.

The first is that of debt counselling and money management. People becoming crippled with debt is an increasing problem in our society. It is a problem which is no respecter class or background. In terms of prevention we hold money management programmes throughout the year. To facilitate debt counselling we have a number of trained counsellors and work with another church nearby to coordinate debt clients. Sometimes the problem of debt is just one of several problems people are facing and so there tends to be ongoing supervision of some clients in other areas such as alcohol dependency and marital relations.

The second area of ministry is providing English as a Second Language Courses (ESL). This has been particularly rewarding in helping those from Eastern European countries, but also from Iran. Three such classes are currently being run. These are ideal settings for conversation about the Christian faith.

The latter area has also been linked in with specific evangelistic outreach to members of the Polish community. We have two Polish Christians who, together with others, have set up a Polish Bible study group which meets fortnightly with the specific aim of explaining the Christian faith. We have also seen increasing numbers of Poles attending our morning service and the text of the sermons is given to them beforehand translated into Polish.

It is important to underscore the willingness to give oneself over to *long term work*. This is not a short sprint; networks take time to be established as well as trust to be gained which gives credibility to what we do. This loops back to something I mentioned earlier when speaking about my upbringing, namely, that from my non-church, antagonistic background there was nonetheless a respect for the Salvation Army. The reason for this is that to miners like my Dad and others raised during the great depression, members of the Salvation Army seemed to care by offering *practical* help. There was the ring of authenticity about what they said because of what they did. Maybe we can learn from that. To be frank, I really can't see how we are going to be reaching people in the 'sink' estates without some form of social involvement and contact. It is then as people's lives are changed through the Gospel that others will be influenced too.

I believe that in order to ensure that any social involvement programme is rooted in the Gospel and leads people to the Gospel, those who are involved, and especially the leaders, should first and foremost be passionate about evangelism. If a desire to 'seek and save the lost' is to the forefront, then the 'mercy' aspect of such ministries will not be lost and neither will be the Gospel intentionality in sharing the faith. If, however, the main focus is solely on 'doing good', then the Gospel sharing aspect will often be eclipsed.

Given the priority of enabling people to hear the Gospel message, it is important that specific evangelistic occasions are created and are ongoing in the church.

From presence to proclamation

The apostle Paul was willing to bring down a curse upon himself if he didn't preach the Gospel. The challenge for us is: Are we willing to bring down such a curse on ourselves if we are not willing to do this in certain social contexts? Evangelicalism today needs to ask the question: are we producing ministers who *will* not or feel they *cannot* minister in such settings? If so that is serious. Paul is clear that it is through presenting the Christian message in the power of the Holy Spirit that people are 'won.' How does that apply in a 'reaching the unreached' setting?

Let me begin by clearing away one or two misconceptions and myths.

The first is the idea that when it comes to preaching, sermons must be dumbed down for the working classes. Certainly we may need to work harder at our preaching in some respects, but that doesn't mean making them patronisingly simple. We are not to confuse lack of education with lack of intelligence! My Dad had next to no formal education but he wasn't stupid. Working men and women can follow an argument although they may need to be helped along a little (indeed, so do many University students today!).

It may come as a surprise to many to learn that Dr Francis Schaeffer came from a very blue collar working class background in Pennsylvania. Colin Duriez writes in his biography of Schaeffer, 'According to his daughter Deborah, the core of Francis Schaeffer's life was there from the beginning: he was "a thinking person who was honest about life." His inherent seriousness did not mean dullness. He enjoyed humour, for instance ... This intense demeanour was not out of keeping with his working-class background. Her father always reckoned, in later life, that there was a deep affinity between the working class person and the intellectual. They shared an honesty in looking at life, whereas the middle classes often lived in a way that was divorced from reality.' [14] That is certainly my experience.

Neither is it the case that such folk can only cope with short sermons. It depends upon who is preaching and how they are preaching. In some cases the problem lies not with the listener but the preacher. It is worth pondering on the fact that ordinary working class men could and would listen to the former National Miners' Union leader, Arthur Scargill for over an hour without any lapse in attention. Why? For one thing he was a gifted orator and the men present were interested in what he had to say—he connected with them. He also used reason as well as humour, and above all he was passionate. All the things one would expect in a Gospel preacher. Certainly, folk may not listen to a lecture, which is what some of our sermons may be turning into, but they will listen to good preachers. And of course we do believe in the work of the Holy Spirit!

In '*The Cities of God*' [15] Stark cites the Belgian historian, Franz Cumont's observation concerning what it was that attracted followers to the oriental religions which came in from the East into the Roman Empire—such as the worship of Cybele and Isis, and in turn paved the way for the reception of Christianity. He noted three things which contrasted them with the pagan religions of Rome: 1.They appealed more strongly to the senses—there was a strong emotional element. 2.They appealed directly to the individual rather than the community, linking faith to conscience and the availability of atonement and 3. They satisfied the intellect. I would suggest all three elements are meant to be found in authentic Christianity and worked out amongst all classes and backgrounds. Some, because of upbringing, shrink back from anything emotional in preaching. This would be a big mistake. If we are going to reach the working classes we need to develop this aspect—as did George Whitefield to great effect. Similarly with the second point, we appeal to the individual. Folk are to be addressed directly so it is *God* speaking to them. And likewise with the third aspect—the use of reason. How this works out will depend upon our context which will mean getting to know what folk can take. I was in a rural church recently which has in the last few years had an evangelical ministry. Very wisely the minister there breaks up the sermon into two parts, separated by a hymn for that is what the folk can take. It will mean being careful in the illustrations we use, using ones which do connect with them and not our ministerial contemporaries—think of the example of Hugh Latimer and his homely style of preaching or the warm logic of George Whitefield (as well as his drama!). We are to aim at engaging the heart and will via the mind.

In order to share the Gospel with as many different people as possible St John's tries to be creative in putting on as many different 'come and see' events as possible. These have included quiz nights, men's games evenings, women's craft nights, as well as what we call 'Spotlight' services on a Sunday with a specific topic dealt with evangelistically. Different types of events to interest different people. We also hold family events which tend to be the biggest draw for the unchurched.

One very important initiative we have undertaken which combines 'come and see' with 'go and tell' evangelism is the 'Identity Course.' This is a specially designed course which uses John's Gospel to explain the Gospel. It runs for seven weeks and the DVD produced was professionally filmed at St John's with evangelist, Lee McMunn. At the outset folk are told that 'nothing is assumed and everything will be explained' which is exactly what happens. This is one of the most accessible evangelistic courses I have come across and has such a wide appeal. We have seen students, professionals, Polish and non-book culture folk come to faith through this course. It is also very flexible to use. It can be downloaded onto a smart phone and used 'one to one' or in homes.

We have found it especially beneficial to use in the homes of those who are enquiring about baptism for their children. It has subtitles in Polish, Farsi, Russian, Spanish and Chinese.[16] This has been wonderfully used by God to lead many to Christ.

The point I want to stress is that in the call for God's people to be 'salt' declaring, 'light' showing, 'city' distinctive people, whatever social involvement there may be (and needs to be), enabling people to hear the Gospel message is to be uppermost in our minds and hearts. Prayer and thought are to be combined which will lead people to the Saviour.

Cultural challenges and Change of hearts

Our context of living in a postmodern culture brings with it new challenges but the Gospel remains the same as does the call for God's people to be different. The challenge has been clearly put by David Wells,[17] 'The postmodern reaction against Enlightenment dogma will not be met successfully simply by Christian proclamation. Of that we can be sure. That proclamation must arise within a context of *authenticity*. It is only as the evangelical Church begins to put its own house in order, its members begin to disentangle themselves from all those cultural habits which militate against a belief in truth, and begin to embody that truth in the way that the Church actually lives, that postmodern scepticism might begin to be overcome. Postmoderns want to see as well as hear, to find authenticity in relationship as the precursor to hearing what is said. This is a valid and biblical demand. Faith, after all, is dead without works, and few sins are dealt with as harshly by Jesus as hypocrisy. What postmoderns want to see, and are entitled to see, is believing and being, talking and doing, all joined together in a seamless whole.'[18]

Kevin Vanhoozer issues a similar challenge: 'It is the church's role to be a light to the nations. The church should be the model for the right use of human freedom; the church should be the civilized society par excellence. The community of believers represents a prophetic counterculture that challenges the gods and myths of the day with regard to which world and life view best fulfils humanity. The church's challenge will only be as strong as its expression of the biblical world and life view … this is not only a matter of correct doctrine but also a matter of faithful biblical performance. The church must be the cultural incarnation of the story of God in Christ.'[19] In other words, the church community in whatever cultural context it finds itself should demonstrate the effects of the Gospel in proclamation and practice.

Let me end by relating just one personal account which illustrates many of the things that have been said.

A while ago I was praying quite earnestly in the staff meeting that God would so move by his Spirit as to convict people who have nothing to do with the church. In true Augustinian style I was asking God that they would be so restless and unhappy until they started to seek after him. That very afternoon I received a phone call from a man who assured me that he wasn't 'nuts' but was quite sane, however, for the life of him he couldn't sleep at night because he was afraid of dying. He simply could not get death out of his mind. He said that he didn't really believe in God, but if God did exist, might this be some way that he was trying to get his attention? He asked if I could help him. And so he came around the following day. He was not very tall, but well built—he came third in the 'Mr Hull' competition some years ago.

He then told me his story.

At 14 he left home and took up with living with a prostitute. At 16 he was sent to prison for attempted murder—he tortured a man by tying him to a lamp post, dousing him in petrol and setting fire to him. Although a big fellow, he had to take out a restraining order on his first wife because she used to beat him up and stubbed out cigarettes on their baby daughter. They got divorced and he moved away with his ten year old son and young daughter. One night his ex-wife came around and the son answered the door (he was about seven years old at the time), she stabbed him and left him in a pool of blood. Thankfully he survived. She then came upstairs brandishing a knife towards this fellow. He then picked up the TV and hit her with it! He was put in jail for that.

Since then he has remarried a much younger woman, has a baby daughter and is a 'landlord'—he has a number of properties around Hull. In fact a more accurate description would be that of an 'Enforcer' as he told me that his approach to his tenants is that if they ever get behind in their rent, he gives them five minutes to come up with the money or he breaks their hands! He was also busy supplying half the cannabis in the City. And he was scared of dying!

So we chatted about God, Christ, the Gospel and I asked if I could pray for him, which I did. In fact, he said, please 'brainwash me to make me feel better'. I said that God could do better than that; he could give a new mind and new heart. Over the following few weeks we met to do the 'Identity Course'.

By week three he was saying he had ever been so happy in his life. He said that he now knew there *was* a God, and that the Bible made sense and everything was looking different. He told me that he discovered that he actually has a conscience!

By the final session he was thoroughly converted and changed beyond recognition.

We continued to meet. Bearing in mind that this is someone with no advanced education and from the toughest and largest housing estate in Hull, he arrived one day and asked if I had heard of someone called 'Calvin' (I wasn't sure if it was Calvin Klein he was asking after!)—*John* Calvin, he told me. I asked why? He enthusiastically informed me that he saw a set of his Bible commentaries 'on line' and had bought them all. What is more, he was reading them with vigour—and understanding them. This was followed by buying a job lot of Luther's sermons!

He is now doing a Bible correspondence course.

He then said, 'If Christ died for *me*, then there is nothing that Christ can ask of me which is ever going to be too much.' He wants to live out his life in sheer gratitude to Christ and is desperate to tell others about him. He remarked that it felt like he had come out of darkness into bright light. He had never read Colossians 1:13 but he has experienced it.

May the Lord grant to us more people like this as Christians unashamedly act as salt in declaring the Gospel, light in seeking to do good to all men, and churches act as cities on hills, being countercultural and distinctive communities amidst a 'crooked and perverse generation'.

ENDNOTES

1. Tim Chester, *Unreached—growing Churches in working-class and deprived areas,* (Leicester: IVP, 2012), p. 1

2. Karl Marx, and Friedrich Engels, *Marx and Engels on Religion.* New York, 1976. p. 316.

3. E. A. Judge, *The Social patterns of Christian groups in the First century.* (London: Tyndale, 1960), p. 52.

4. Rodney Stark, *The Rise of Christianity. A Sociologist Reconsiders History,* (Princeton, 1996).

5. D. A. Carson, 'Pauline Inconsistency', *Churchman,* Vol 100, No 1, 1986.

6. Rodney Stark and Roger Finke, *Acts of Faith, Explaining the Human side of Religion,* (University of California Press, 2000), Chapter 5.

7. Ibid. p. 122.

8. Ibid. p. 137.

9. Stark, *The Rise of Christianity,* p. 161.

10. Ibid. p. 82

11. Thucydides, *The Peloponnesian War* (London: Penguin, 1954), 51-53.

12. Quoted in Starke, *The Rise of Christianity,* p. 84

13. Kate Fox, *Watching the English: The Hidden Rules of English Behaviour,* (London: Hodder and Stoughton, 2005)

14. Colin Duriez, *Francis Schaeffer, an Authentic Life,* (Leicester: IVP, 2008) p. 19.

15. Rodney Stark, *Cities of God. The real story of how Christianity became an urban movement and conquered Rome,* (San Francisco: Harper Press, 2006), p. 86.

16. 'The Identity Course' published by '10ofthose'.

17. David F Wells, '*Above all earthly Powers—Christ in the Post Modern World.*' (Leicester: IVP, 2006).

18. Ibid. p. 315.

19. Kevin Vanhoozer, 'The World Well Staged.', *First Theology* (Nottingham: Apollos, 2002), p. 334